Totally Ted! 2

With My
Warmest Best Wishes

Ted Shovell

Totally Ted! 2

More Witty Reflections on Modern Life from a Grumpy Old Westcountry Man

TED SHERRELL

Illustrations by
Becky Sheppard

UNITED WRITERS
Cornwall

UNITED WRITERS PUBLICATIONS LTD
Ailsa, Castle Gate, Penzance, Cornwall.
www.unitedwriters.co.uk

British Library Cataloguing in Publication Data:
A catalogue record for this book is
available from the British Library.

ISBN 9781852001889

Printed and bound in Great Britain by
United Writers Publications Ltd.,
Cornwall.

To my lovely Ann,
the 'rock' upon which I have built my life,
and to our enchanting family,
now into a third generation,
who bring such fulfilment to our world.

The *Totally Ted!* columns originally appeared
fortnightly in the Tavistock, Okehampton, East
Cornwall and Princetown Times newspapers.

Contents

1

The Pressure Washer

WE are blessed, Ann and I, with a wonderful family –
kind, thoughtful, caring; they are pure gold. This has
long been the case but, as we move ever deeper into
mature years, their support for us has grown even more
and rarely does it ever have to be requested.

Such was exemplified recently when we asked our
grandson, Tom, to suggest whom we could contact to
come, accompanied by a machine, to cleanse our paths
and patio, all shrouded, unaccountably, by levels of grime
which could feature in a Lowry painting. Instantly he gave
us a name – his own. He would hire the relevant machine
and would, one weekend, come along and return our
concrete and paving slabs to pristine condition. We did not
hesitate in our acceptance of such generosity of spirit and
effort.

Thus, on a Sunday morning a couple of weeks later did
he appear, along with his father – our son James, who was
transporting the pressure washer in his van. A largish,
exceedingly heavy brute, it was placed in the relevant
position to commence the assault on the footpaths. So far,

so good. All that needed doing was to connect the power, plus the water supply, to the blue-coloured beast and battle would commence.

To be fair there was not the slightest problem with laying on the electrics – a wandering lead caused a light to beam promisingly from the side of the washer; once the water supply was attached, it would be all systems go. This, though, was not quite as simple or straight forward as anticipated. Our hose reel, though ancient and a touch crinkled, was sufficiently long to reach from tap to appliance; the problem was, however, that once it arrived there, the situation was somewhat similar to that which confronted so many fire brigades who went to the assistance of the city of Plymouth during the Blitz (though somewhat less calamitous). Simply the connection on the end of the reel would not fit onto the relevant protuberance on the side of the washer. There followed fiddling with accessories, to no avail, then discussion and finally head scratching (practical idiot that I am, I was both pleased and relieved to be able to join in the last of these exercises).

Fortunately James is a man of good common sense and hands-on ability; always good in crises, great or small. Off he went to his home nearby and was soon back with a couple of attachments he'd found in a box of multiple odds and ends. The first was the wrong size, but the second did fit – well, almost anyway. It was slightly loose and assuredly would fly off under pressure.

Thus did he, producing a pair of pliers, pull it here, twist it there, break off a piece causing an obstruction – and solve the problem. All that was needed now was the water; thus I was sent down to the back of the house to turn on

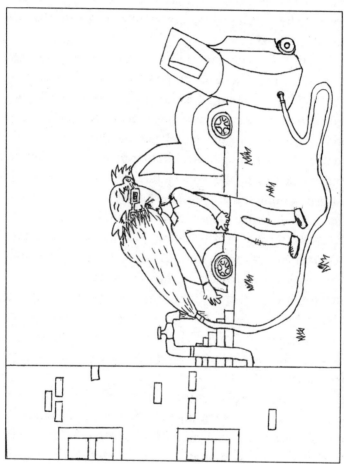

Once the water supply was attached, it would be all systems go!

the hose bearing tap. The handle was duly turned and the good news was that South West Water were fulfilling their basic function – the clear, cold liquid was cascading from the tap. There was though, in this, a slight problem – it was supposed to be hurtling along our veteran hose towards the nozzle of the washer.

The reality? The pressure had forced the pipe from the source; once more a halt to proceedings and again a scratching of the cranium, this time led by myself. My son inspected the connection and stated that the jubilee clip around it was rusted and could not be tightened to the degree needed. Looking at the circular band in question, it became apparent why the word 'jubilee' was used as clearly it had been purchased at the time of the Queen's Diamond Jubilee – Victoria that is, not Elizabeth the Second.

Over two hours of frustration had passed since the commencement of the attempt to eliminate the grime and not a solitary drip of water had been fired from the business end of the squat, muscular appliance. Now, if it had been left to me, I would have uttered a two word phrase – the second being 'it', the first being optional but usually containing six letters or fewer – then gone indoors to read the paper.

My son and grandson, though, imbued with the tenacious resilience which made Britain great, hurtled off in the van once more, returning some 20 minutes later with the crucial clip. It was attached and, despite some water squirting out from around it, sufficient reached the nozzle for the job to be completed – most successfully. However, it is hard to ignore one depressing thought – it will have to be done again next year!

2

The Mail Order

*I*T was Ann who espied it when glancing through one of the many catalogues, which bursts through, regularly, our letter box – virtually all, fortunately, addressed to her. Intently she gazed at a page for a couple of minutes, then passed it to me.

'That could be a good buy,' she said; her judgement on such matters is usually first class, never giving anything consideration unless it is something we need, pleases the eye and appears good value. I looked down at a picture of a pair of suitcases – large and medium – on special offer; in an attractive and bright claret colour. Immediately I could see what she meant; our luggage, while sound, have been around a while and are getting shabby. Possibly more relevant, though, they are black – and we are getting older, our eyesight likewise. Thus in airports, when standing alongside 'carousels' searching for cases just disgorged from an aircraft, it has been increasingly difficult to pick out ours amongst what, often, is a sea of darkness.

Quite recently, I grabbed what appeared our property – and almost suffered a hernia. Whose it was, I know not, but its weight was such it could have held a dismembered corpse; yet it looked so very much like our larger one. If it had been of a distinctive – preferably bright – hue then no mistake would have been made. With all this in mind, it was easy for us to make a decision; credit card in hand, I headed for the phone.

My call was answered quickly – or to be more accurate, a voice which sounded a touch like a female Dalek listed several options. Choosing the only one which mentioned sales, I was informed my call could be used for 'training purposes' (unlikely with my slurred old Devonshire accent), then had the ear caressed with Mozart; not so melodic was the tone of the lady who kept informing me that 'Your call is important to us', though clearly not so vital that they worry they might lose a potential customer who refuses to waste good money, and time, waiting with ever increasing impatience at the end of the phone.

The handset about to be slammed down on the receiver, a human voice, male, suddenly asked how he could help. He was pleasant and efficient, so the deal was done, the goods paid for by card and even arrangements made for the delivery to be left in the shed should there be nobody at home. So far, so good.

Unfortunately, matters go downhill from this moment on. For, a week or so later, we arrived home just before lunch – on a rainy day – not to find our suitcases stored in the shed, but left on the doorstep in the wet. Actually this is not totally accurate, for only one case was there – the larger of the two ordered; we took the box indoors. Opening it we gazed down at a smart looking piece of luggage; one problem, though – the colour, if we were planning a manoeuvre through enemy lines, then no problem, it being of a khaki hue; assuredly it was not the bright claret we ordered. Thus the phone saga – episode two.

The music again was pleasant but not the wisest choice as it alluded to time – the *Minute Waltz*. It had played in my ear at least half a dozen times before I was able to air my grievance. A charming lady took full details, apologised, profusely, and assured me that the rogue case would be collected within a few days, the correct one left in its place.

On reflection, she did it with a confident aplomb which suggested she spent most of her working life soothing unhappy customers. Reassuringly, her promise appeared to have been kept, for a few days later we returned home to find the offending case collected and a new one left in its place (though why the fresh one was again placed on the doorstep when the other was gathered from the outhouse will be forever a mystery). The box was gathered up in welcoming arms, borne inside, and opened; hope abounded. It was to be dashed; for whilst a pristine case lay within, it still bore a colour more useful to the SAS than ourselves; indeed, it could well have been the same one we had returned.

Back to the phone; this time it was Scott Joplin playing *Rag Time* – it should have been *Abide With Me*. Eventually a human voice. Tersely, but as politely as I could manage, I explained the catalogue of calamity since first lodging our order. Instantly, I was mollified – a full refund was offered, and accepted with alacrity. Thus ended the drama. Or has it? For somewhere, there is a second valise from the original order which has never appeared; hopefully, it never will. The phone bill would be astronomical.

3

Work – Blessing or Curse?

'BLESSED is he who has found his work – let him ask no other blessedness.' So wrote Thomas Carlyle, the eminent 19th century Scottish essayist and philosopher. Certainly a bold statement – one with which it is possible to take issue. Is not good health the supreme 'blessedness' – a long life where visits to doctors and hospitals are as rare as the coming of Halley's Comet?

Personal matters, too, of course; a close, loving relationship with a spouse or partner, a rich, rewarding family life – are these not vital to happiness, contentment and an overall feeling of well being?

Yet, it is difficult to argue that there is much in Carlyle's words; one may ask for 'other blessedness', such as winning the lottery, or to be following, at long last, a permanently successful Plymouth Argyle team; but to rise in the morning looking forward to one's work (or, at least, not dreading the prospect) is something to be valued. After all, most of us of both genders will spend a large proportion of our lives earning a living; thus it helps very considerably if one is earning their crust by doing something they love, or enjoy, or, at the very least, with which they are comfortable. Personally, I have encompassed a wide range of emotion, competence, enthusiasm – or a total lack of them – when seeking my daily bread; some jobs I've heartily disliked, others have brought reasonable satisfaction (especially if they've produced tolerable financial reward). A few I've enjoyed – especially that which I do now, my work for this excellent local newspaper. My problem regarding my working life is that I was not truly – certainly in early years – one 'who has found his work'; thus I have since 1959 – when first, as a teenager, I commenced paid employment – searched for this Holy Grail. That I've spent the past 56 years seeking it – and I have, assuredly, looked in a multitude of directions, some possibly a touch off the beaten (and sensible) track – is one of the reasons I remain in paid employment, even though I've accrued, possibly, as many years as there are hairs on my scalp and assuredly far more than the number of brain cells fighting for survival in this wizened old head.

This 'rolling stone' has gathered little 'moss' over these years, due in no small measure to a persistent feeling over the decades – not always strong, but present nevertheless – that 'the other man's grass is always greener, the sun shines brighter on the other side.' Thus I have earned a living, never princely but generally adequate, in a multitude of roles – as a newspaper reporter, a farm worker, a civil servant, a door-to-door salesman, an office worker, an ice cream salesman, an insurance agent, a shopkeeper, a fireman (full-time and retained), a security guard in a holiday camp plus a number of others, some lasting just a few weeks.

The one major bonus of leading a mercurial – some might say feckless – working life is that material for writing comes one's way in swathes with the tedium of research rarely required (ideal for an idle man); many years on councils and sitting as a magistrate have also produced a bountiful harvest when it comes to the idiosyncrasies, complexities and absurdities of human nature.

The writing of tales – some short, some novel length – has, for me, never been hard; likewise the penning of newspaper articles. What is difficult, however, is being good at it – being able to create that which the many wish to read, not the very few; that which impresses readers and critics alike. Such is the goal to aim for, the level of attainment to seek. Realistically – in moments of cold analysis – I am aware it is the utopia I shall never find; this second division utility player is never going to be a premier league superstar. Yet, perhaps, to a limited degree, some 'blessedness' has come my way in this direction; whether at home or at work, I'm rarely happier than when I have a pen in hand. After all, Carlyle did not state that success and riches – or, indeed, talent – came into the equation; satisfaction, fulfilment, a joy derived from labour – that has to be the goal, the desire.

There are those in this world who know, from childhood, that which they wish to do in life; they are assuredly fortunate; equally certain, they are rare. Sadly there are some folk who shuffle through their lives desiring only retirement. Most of as, though, whilst probably not feeling 'blessed' regarding employment, still feel quite happy; and the money comes in handy as well.

4

Surveys & Statistics

*T*HERE would appear to be numerous folk in this
country employed in research, surveys and compiling
statistics. In principle, there is nothing wrong with this –
the opposite, in fact; for progress can rarely be made
unless problems, especially those of a medical nature, are
analysed in deep, meaningful ways and possible solutions
found; then the path ahead can be signposted to avoid
these and other adversities, prevention always being better
than cure.

The problem is, however, there would seem to be a
chronic lack of unity and consistency plus basic common
sense amongst the ranks of the so called 'experts'. They
produce, with extraordinary regularity, advice for all
(especially in health matters), the following of which they
will say greatly help towards longevity, quality of life plus
prevention of disease and illness.

Alcohol features majorly, the safe amounts to be drunk
varying seemingly according to which day of the week
one reads the papers or absorbs radio and television news.

On the Monday research could well warn against the

imbibing of more than a couple of glasses of red wine a week; someone on Tuesday, though, will state, authoritatively, that it does no harm to have a couple of draughts a day, perhaps more if it is white. Wednesday, however, might well bring dismay to those of us who like the fermented juice of the grape, for there could be stern advice – instruction, even – that the consumption of any alcohol is injurious to the system.

Wise folk will take no notice of this, for there is every chance that Thursday's informed musings might suggest alcohol can be effective in combating 'flus' colds and the like. As for Friday, the zeal of the advisers will be weakening – perhaps it will be deemed acceptable to consume amounts of everything from whisky to wine, beer to cocktails in whatever quantities desired as long as it is not before breakfast. Come the weekends, people can feel free to do exactly what they want – researchers only work a five day week.

Observations from experts and statisticians can get even more bizarre – daft, in fact. Recently it was stated – seemingly officially – that when families with youngish children are travelling longish distances, drivers should be aware of the times when, firstly, boredom sets in, then when the same afflicted child – or plural – becomes 'hot and bothered' (one assumes this refers only to summer months, but such was not stated). The former situation will occur after 2 hours 23 minutes; as to a solution, none is stated; perhaps when that critical moment is reached, the nearest theme park should be located – repercussions of boredom to the health of the child could be immense. As to being hot and bothered – which will occur just 14 minutes later – if the theme park has not been found, then possibly the car should be pulled over onto the hard shoulder and the youngsters allowed to escape into the air. Nonsense? Of course it is; as John McEnroe might have put it, they 'cannot be serious'. Yet one presumes they are, for such idiocies are produced not just for fun; most will be funded by governments or universities and the like and done so in the mind-set of the 'Nanny state' – the conviction of many in the establishment, Civil Service and administration that the stoic people of this great nation cannot be trusted to safeguard our own health, solve our personal problems, live our lives in a sensible, responsible way.

So much of this offends and that which does not irritates – at times, even angers. Quite apart from it being an intrusion into our lives – perhaps even an assault upon our liberties – it represents a scandalous waste of resources, with so much of it being plain daft.

Recently an official report regarding education stated that those youngsters who played truant from school were likely to do less well than students who attended regularly. Really? That is a surprise! A summary regarding violent crime came to the profound conclusion that such tends to be in neighbourhoods where there are found to be the greatest concentration of weapons; a survey concerning the aspiration of young people suggests it tends to be much lower when their parents have little; an astonishing revelation! Another stated that homeowners tended to feel more financially secure than those who rented, whilst a gem was the pronouncement that those poor folk 'living rough' were more likely to contract serious illness than those of us who spent our nights in warm beds – especially in winter; and so it goes on, ad infinitum.

Granted it makes work for somebody but the problem is that so often such pointless exercises are funded from the long suffering tax payers; it exasperates – to say the least.

5

Village Life

OF all the futile exercises that can be indulged there are few more pointless than looking back to one's earlier years with nostalgia. No harm in remembering the past, mind you – especially the mistakes made; after all, if one does not recall, and learn, then they are destined to be repeated. However, it is surely important not to compare then and now in critical fashion, but rather to note the differences for good or ill – and each era possesses both.

What we are talking here, essentially, is social history, the constant shifting sands of human behaviour, beliefs, priorities, ways of life, character, prejudice, ambitions and desires.

I was born, bred and brought up on the Bere Peninsula back in the 1940s and 50s. It was a tight knit, largely self sufficient community, with many of the families having dwelt there for generations; assuredly the transience of people in this day and age was not to be found. Such was true of many rural parishes, but being a peninsula, Bere was probably more insular than most. The bulk of the needs of residents of the villages and hamlets, plus the economically important farming and horticultural entities, were met. To be found were a butcher, baker, barber, post office, grocer, pub, newsagent, fish and chip shop, chemists, taxi, blacksmith, coal merchant, church, chapels and so much more, including a main line railway station, which made up, to some extent, for the poorish roads – and there was a film show in the parish hall, weekly. Thus the satisfactory cohesiveness of the parish was down to the contributions of many.

Looking back, though, there were three locals who, possibly, were more pivotal to the welfare of the citizenry than others – those who looked after the body, the soul and the law. The first was in the hands of an able doctor who, being an ex-Army medic, assumed that anyone reasonably young seeking his help was usually malingering; so sympathy from him was rare. Mind you, he had little time for such as he was a 'one-man band' – no partners, receptionists, nurses or the like; his surgery was in his own house along with a waiting room to which one went, without making an appointment, if needing his professional advice. On rare occasions he would have a locum, but most of the time he was on call 24/7 (in modern jargon).

Matters of faith were, to an extent, the province of the Church of England rector. However, unlike the doctor he was not alone in administering to the spiritual needs of a diverse local populace with a healthy percentage of sinners. For whilst he was the representative of the established church, the peninsula was strong non-conformist country; there were about the parish no fewer than five chapels in the care of two ministers – Methodist and Congregational.

The vicar, though, was 'a character'; often this description can bestow upon someone a better image than

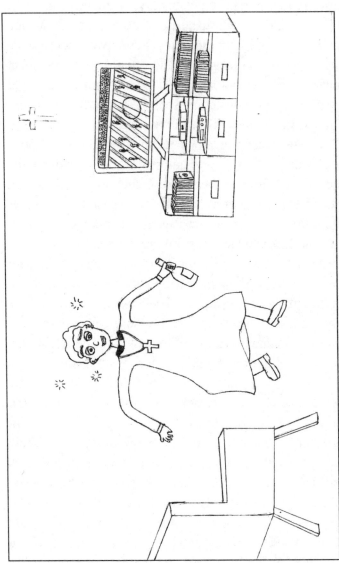

The vicar, though, was 'a character' – with no small measure of eccentricity.

b

they deserve, but in this gentleman's case it was a positive word to portray a man of personality, originality, integrity, geniality – with no small measure of eccentricity. In an age when 'men of the cloth' (and they were always men) were so often 'tee-total', this gent would often frequent the local hostelries, did the football pools on a regular basis and enjoyed dancing and watching sport. What further endeared him to his 'flock', was his power as a preacher. Those were the days when congregations relished articulate sermons voiced with passion – especially those delivered on the subject of 'hellfire and damnation'; such appealed to Non Conformists particularly; thus did, on occasions, a number of them forsake chapel services to attend the Anglican church and listen to the vicar 'giving them hell!'

As to law and order, most villages had their own policeman, the actual station usually being in the house where dwelt the officer and his family. The constable on the peninsula was posted there as a relatively young man during the 1930s and remained until his retirement in the early 1960s.

His was a 'light touch on the tiller' when it came to law enforcement; a zealot he was not. He seemed to be possessing of a philosophy that a 'blind eye' could often be turned towards activities which, whilst not strictly in accordance with statute, did little harm to anyone else. He would have written so rarely in his official notebook, it is doubtful he ever used more than one during his career. Yet, nearly always, was he able to keep the peace.

There is no police house – or officer – on the peninsula now, and whilst a rector remains in residence, medical cover comes from Tavistock; the realities of modern life yes – but progress?

26

6

The Flight

*I*T was a present, greatly appreciated, from Ann and the family for my birthday back in December, but I only got around to enjoying it in June.

The main reason for such delay was that it could only successfully be activated when weather conditions were kind. The gift? An hour's flight in a small aircraft based on a remote airfield in mid-Cornwall – a chance to view, from above, areas of the Duchy, especially the north coast, where we have enjoyed, over the decades, so many relaxing holidays.

Arrangements for the event to take place were relatively easy to make – we are not talking Heathrow here; my phone call was answered by a fellow who, sounding a touch flustered, asked me to 'hold on a minute'; good to his word, some 60 seconds later he was back on the line. 'Sorry about that,' he said, 'but I'm in the hangar at the moment sorting out an engine and I needed to wipe some of the oil off my hands. How can I help?' Speedily I told him and within 90 seconds the flight was booked for 10am on an upcoming Saturday morning; matters had been set in motion.

The voucher permitted me to take two guests; Ann had done the flight before, so I was to be accompanied by my son David – who usually 'draws the short straw' of taking me to Home Park – and daughter-in-law Penny, wife of James. So we were geared up for a timely start on a sunny summer morning – one which became even earlier.

For the evening before the day of the epic odyssey, I received a phone call from a lady at the airfield; she asked if it was possible for us to arrive there half an hour earlier, as they had taken a booking from a gent of an amorous nature who intended to write, in the sand on a beach near Padstow, a proposal of marriage to his girlfriend, then be flown over it for her to make reply.

An innovative plan, indeed, but one which could only work at about 11am as not long after this hour, the tide, lamentably lacking romance, would rapidly wash this loving question into oblivion. 'Miserable Toad' though I am, I had not the heart to turn down such a request – thus an hour earlier was set for our journey down the A30.

We arrived at the airfield in good time; the weather seemed perfect – bright sunshine, sparse cloud, no wind. We were surrounded by acres of grass of varying lengths, some of it cut to form undulating runways; close by lay modest, mature hangars and admin buildings plus a goodly number of planes, either small or minute, a few of which might well have had starring roles in that hilarious film of long ago *Those Magnificent Men In Their Flying Machines*.

We were greeted by a pleasant lady, then the pilot – a most affable gent. However, his message was not positive. 'We've got a problem,' said he. Now granted these words had not the gravity of those from the space shuttle many years ago, 'Houston, we have a problem', but they were mind concentrating none the less.

It appeared – bizarrely to us – that because there was virtually no breeze, the aircraft, a Cessna, would have difficulty taking off with four of us on board; in silence he indicated the plane standing some 50 yards away, which looked as if it might have been around long before the first Spitfire and was so small that one felt it could well have difficulty rising from the ground if it was merely transporting a couple of hamsters.

Thus it was suggested that as it was my present, I did the hour while Penny and David had half an hour each (a brace of take-offs and landings). This was agreed – when 'needs must' as the saying goes. What did not receive assent, however, was the suggestion from the pilot, that, under his supervision, I take the controls for much of the time. No thanks. I did not come all that way to do the driving; anyway, I would be a menace in the air.

Thus did Dave assist on the first trip, and Penny on the second (both with aplomb), whilst I lounged on the back seat and enjoyed the inspirational views; the undulating landscape back from the sea, then that bleak, but inspirational north coast – and the beaches, of course, upon one of which was scrawled, in defiance of the malevolent ocean, 'Amanda, will you marry me?' Twice did I make this journey in the hour – so magnificent it is, that ten times could not be too much.

Thank you, my lovely Ann and family, for such a great gift. Something we never found out though – did Amanda say yes?

7

Education & Know-how

*B*EING a man with the common sense and practical
ability of a half-witted donkey, and aware at my age it
is far too late for me to improve, I never cease to wonder at
the skills and acumen of those people in the world who, when
confronted with technical problems, are able to solve them –
often quickly, efficiently and with a minimum of fuss.

Mind you, to achieve a high level of academic
education is to be both admired and respected; yet rightly
or wrongly, it seems to me that a goodly percentage of the
population, if diligent, dedicated and determined, can
achieve reasonable levels in this direction. To restore a
central heating boiler to health, however, or to pinpoint the
fault which causes an electrical trip to be activated with
frustrating regularity, and to be able to put it right – these
to me are talents bordering on genius.

Then there is the revival of life to a moribund 'infernal
combustion engine' to quote the words of Sir Winston
Churchill; a Ferrari is less use than a wheelbarrow if the
motor won't start.

This was a situation brought home to me a few years

ago when we were on holiday in Wales – not riding in an excessively expensive Italian car, I hasten to add, but rather a weary Austin Allegro. I pulled the vehicle into a filling station in tranquil countryside near a village with numerous 'Ls' in the title, the petrol gauge jammed on 'empty'.

Having filled the thirsty tank, I went into the garage, duly paid for it, then returned to the car, got in and attempted to restart it – notably without success. I turned the engine but it showed no desire to come to life. Realising the battery would soon be beggared, I stopped – then saw standing beside the wretched machine the welcoming presence of the mechanic who had taken payment for the fuel. He signalled me to open the bonnet. Having released the catch, I joined him as he lifted it then gazed down at the engine; to me it was a motley collection of metal, but to him, clearly, it resembled a keyboard upon which he was about to play a melody.

He reached down, pushed a button here, twisted a screw there, clouted something else, then said: 'Try her now.'

With alacrity, I jumped back into the driver's seat; turned the ignition key – and the engine burst into glorious life. I alighted, thanked him profusely then enquired as to how much I owed for his 'magical' touch.

'A pound and a penny,' was his reply. 'A penny for doing it, but a pound for knowing how to.' In reality he took nothing for his act of salvation – but I have never forgotten those profound words. Knowledge of how to put right the breakdowns, mishaps, technical and practical deficiencies, mistakes – indeed, calamities – which can so terrorise we of little nous, bereft of pragmatic learning and aptitude, is 'beyond rubies'; to have a friend, contact, colleague, relation – or, indeed, to know a professional who will turn out promptly for a fair fee – when the abyss of mechanical and structural catastrophe looms at one's feet with no warning (usually the case); well, I find it hard to articulate words which, accurately, reflect my admiration and esteem for such gifted folk.

Unfairly, indeed shamefully, in modern life the dexterily gifted and innovative, those adept at building or repairing the creations, objects and structures which bring sophistication, comfort and the sense of wellbeing to our lives, all too often are not afforded the respect and status (or salaries) accorded to someone who, say, has been to university, or can string a few letters after their name. These often obscure symbols might mean the holder has a degree in Scottish dancing or a qualification in origami or the like; no harm in this – and clearly there are many academic attainments of crucial value in the world. For sure our civilisation would ultimately collapse if they did not exist. Indeed, most of us make some useful contribution to society thanks to our common sense, knowledge, learning and abilities (though I must concede that my value is minimal – a modest awareness of English history, an addiction to the exploits of Sherlock Holmes plus a consciousness of the promotion seasons of Plymouth Argyle – a shortish list – does little to aid mankind).

However, when the tempest blows, the floods engulf, the pipes freeze, the roads are blocked, the roof is ripped, the area is blacked out, communications fail as the 'system crashes' – or, simply, the television won't work – it is those splendid folk able to combine perception with practical skills plus a dollop of gumption to whom we turn often in desperation.

8

The Visit

*I*T was a sound coming from a distance – possibly east of Dartmoor; it could have been a rumble of thunder, but Ann and I knew otherwise. Also we were aware it would get louder – inexorably. It was not a noise to alarm – not the drone of enemy aircraft or the like; rather an ever increasing cacophony of happiness and exuberance.

The level of decibels suggested Okehampton had been reached – passed, in fact; it rose ever higher and more penetrating – to such a pitch it almost drowned out the wailing sirens of a passing fire engine. We had no doubts that Tavistock had been reached, thus did we thrust ajar our front door (following a liberal ingesting of suitably soothing medicine – in my case, a decent single malt), then stood like statues just outside, awaiting our fate. Close now was the leviathan dominating our hearing – a quarter of a mile away at the most; then, suddenly, the bedlam was alongside our abode – and not moving away. They had been expected, and had arrived; as was anticipated, they had not crept up on us – such is not their way.

The gate at the top of the longish path burst open, and a

tsunami of children (only three in reality but a classful could not have made a more dramatic entrance) hurtled towards us with shrieks of joy (well, I assume that's what they were).

They were greeted by grandparents who, whilst a touch more sedate, were delighted and relieved to see them – also their parents, who followed a little more slowly down the path; son and daughter-in-law, Matthew and Avisa, had forsaken the sunshine (and humidity) of Hong Kong and were back in the 'Old Country' for a brief spell and were to spend a few days staying with us along with their rowdy progeny.

There was an almost overwhelming aura of mutuality – we were all so pleased, even overjoyed to see each other; for it had been a year almost to the day since last we had been together, the old Crown Colony in the South China Seas having been their home and place of employment for quite a while now. Lost time, assuredly, was tackled with enthusiasm – 12 months cannot be easily bridged in six days, but a valiant attempt was made by all. Ann had prepared a series of sumptuous feasts, wine flowed in abundance (fortunately the children didn't fancy it), the sun shone reasonably kindly – by Devon standards, at least – goodwill was all around. The full awareness of just how much people are missed surely only becomes fully apparent when one is reunited with them – when the void is filled – albeit briefly. Many members of the wider family came to call, others were visited – warmth, fellowship and love was in abundance; sadly time passed all too rapidly.

On the Saturday, though, son Matthew ensured there was a change of tone. Like his father, he can on occasions have something of the puritan about him; life at times may be a 'bowl of cherries' but it is a rare one which does not suffer spasms of pain. On that day Matt felt it was time to show his offspring the darker side of existence. He, like us, has brought up his daughters and son to honour their father and mother – and to follow Plymouth Argyle. Due largely to their longish period in the Far East, none of them had ever made the pilgrimage to Home Park; this was to be rectified. After a largish lunch (the traumas to come were not to be faced on an empty stomach), the children were forcibly bedecked in the sacred green, then they, their parents – plus hapless grandparents – headed south towards the great dockyard city.

The trip was made more in hope than expectation – well, for the adult members of the party, that is. On the return journey some three hours later, silence reigned – even the ebullient youngsters were without voice; Argyle had lost 0-3, and, to quote the legendary Brian Clough, 'they were lucky to get nil.' There is, of course, time yet for their long term mental wellbeing – they might well exercise wisdom beyond their years and support another team; but they had best not let their dad and grandad hear of it. One bonus, though, was that the evening meal was devoured in relative silence. It was not to last – next morning normality had returned; youthful vitality ruled.

The day following this – a more sombre mood; farewells were said, hugs and kisses exchanged, an occasional tear shed. Heathrow would be the next step for the family – and a flight to New York, their new location; an invitation to visit next spring was issued; it was accepted – for we do miss them.

9

Remembrance

'*H*AVE you forgotten yet? . . . Look down and swear by the slain of the war that you'll never forget.' From his poem *Aftermath*, lines penned by brave soldier and acclaimed poet Sigfried Sassoon of the four, plus, calamitous years of the second decade of the 20th century that traumatised so much of the world – The Great War.

Unlike vast numbers of others (including many fine writers and artists) he came through it and lived for almost half a century more, but his considerable and estimable literary works were ever influenced by those traumatic times. It is probable he would have been pleased that throughout those years the people of this nation did not forget. Now, virtually another five decades since his demise, it might possibly surprise him that more than 100 years after the beginning of that first great conflict of the last century, the sacrifice, suffering, ordeals and valiance of so many British men and women – military and civilian alike – remains to the forefront of minds, including those of the younger generations. Now, of course, we remember much more than the likes of the Somme and

Passchendaele – the brutal slaughter of the First World War – though this dreadful conflict brought grief to virtually every family in the land.

In my own, my great uncle was wounded three days before the Armistice and died three days after; he never saw his only child. Some solace came to folk when it was suggested they had just fought, and won, 'the War to End All Wars'. Was ever a platitudinous promise more grotesquely mocked? For in little more than two decades following the falling silent of the guns in Flanders, the bloodiest, most destructive conflict in history began; it was to last for six ruinous years.

Uniquely Britain was the only nation to be involved in the Second World War from its eruption in September 1939, when we confronted the vicious Nazis of Hitler's Germany, until August 1945 when the brutal Japanese Empire finally surrendered. It was a conflagration which, it has been calculated, cost some 70 million lives worldwide (military and civilian), saw vast numbers homeless, and left Europe awash with legions of displaced people and refugees. Britain, though victorious, was left bankrupt, so many of our cities half destroyed, large numbers of our civilian population dead.

Stonemasons were hardly able to cope with the Herculean task of chiselling onto thousands of war memorials throughout the land, erected to the fallen of the 1914-18 war, the host of a following generation who had perished fighting for King and Country in this second global struggle.

It is of some comfort that in the 70 plus years since, there have been no wars remotely of such magnitude, but there have been conflicts by the score, and the armed forces of this nation have been involved in them probably more than those of any other; statistics give support to this, for throughout the past 100 years there has been just one when a member of the military of this land was not killed in action.

There were the bitter hostilities versus the vast, merciless Chinese Army in Korea during the early 1950s, numerous involvements in our old colonial territories in the 1960s, the nightmare scenario of trying to keep order, for so many years, in Northern Ireland, the regaining of the Falkland Islands from the invading Argentinians in the 1980s.

Our forces have been involved, often, in trying to keep peace – and defend the vulnerable – throughout the globe; while in more recent times our troops have seen action, and suffered considerable casualties (many killed) in such places as the Gulf, Iraq and Afghanistan; here they have had to fight terrorists and the like who did not – and do not – adhere to the Geneva Convention, which must have been as debilitating mentally as physically.

A Spanish diplomat, at the time of the Falklands War, referred to we British as 'A Warrior Race'. As his country supported the Argentine regime, it is doubtful he meant those comments as a compliment; yet, one feels it should be taken as such. For the inhabitants of our islands are natural warriors – and ever have been. For almost a millennium, we have repulsed all potential invaders, while in more recent times our fine fighting forces have been globe trotters defending the weak against oppressors.

Granted this has not always been the case, but it is

surely arguable that the freedom enjoyed by so many, especially in Western Europe, owes much to the steadfastness and courage of our race. The sacrifice, though, has been immense; and it is this large numbers will recall when we stand in silence, heads bowed, this Remembrance Sunday.

So rest easy, Mr Sassoon – we have not forgotten; nor will we.

Mail & Maserati

*T*HOSE reliable, hard working ladies and gentlemen of the Royal Mail have, over the decades, provided Ann and myself with a service of the highest calibre.

No matter what the weather (and we get a lot of that in Tavistock) they have wended their way down our longish path – then up again, of course – to bring us copious amounts of a manifold range of correspondence much of which keeps us abreast with what is happening in the world.

It was a journey they had to make most days in the past – few were letter free. This was down largely to my long term involvement with a brace of councils; occasionally the envelopes would arrive singly, but there were times when they would penetrate the letterbox in shoals, usually large and buff, varying in thickness from the wafer thin to those possessing the volume and weight of a concrete block. Contained would be memos, agendas, reports, comments, lists of plans, strategic visions, complaints, glossy reports from outside bodies and 'quangos' minutes of committees and the like – an ocean of paperwork. The bulk of it had probably little interest to even the most zealous of councillors (which assuredly, I was not), and contained little of importance or relevance. However, these myriad sheets had to be perused, for somewhere there might be a paragraph or sentence of real pertinence to the lives of local council taxpayers.

This ceased just under two years ago with my retirement from public life; thus the journeys of Royal Mail personnel to our door have been reduced by half – and the weight of mail by two thirds; Ann gets more than I do these days – not something I find disappointing. There's still a tidy amount, mind you, including the inevitable bill, sporadic postcard and such like – and on occasions, even a personal letter, though in this texting and email age such are an endangered species. Mostly, however, it is what is so often termed – perhaps a little unfairly – 'junk mail'.

Granted the regular flow of glossy brochures, booklets even, exhorting one to upgrade broadband, purchase the latest mobile, double glaze everything from the front door to the cat flap, insure against a multitude of calamities (some exceedingly obscure), have eyes and/or ears tested, invest savings (at present interest rates, the bookies are probably more rewarding than the banks), support charities and the like – can be annoying, but the majority are redirected to the recycling bin without the hassle of being opened. Also, it is a fact that were it not for the income that Royal Mail derive from this type of communication, the price of stamps for 'serious' correspondence, high enough as it is, would be astronomical; further to this positive aspect of such postal deliveries a recent invasion of our letter box lifted my spirits considerably – and my ego.

Unusually these days, a torrent of missives hit the

doormat, four of them addressed to me; there was a bill, but fortunately relatively small so it was put aside for payment without argument or dispute; next to be perused was a suggestion from local undertakers that I pre-pay for my funeral. Instantly this was recycled, unopened, as we are both of the view that any savings we have accrued are far more beneficial to our future lying in our account rather than that of funeral directors.

The third was from a cruise ship company suggesting we avail ourselves of a leisurely trip, at what seemed a reasonable price, around the Norwegian fjords. There was a minus though, temperature wise as well as anything else; for the cruise was to happen in January – bitterly cold; with about half an hour's natural light per day; recycling, again.

The final one, clearly, was advertising also – but addressed to me using my first name rather than an initial; in boldish lettering on the envelope was marked – 'Maserati'. I gazed in astonishment; granted our battered Honda Jazz needs replacing – but a Maserati? Perhaps, at last, I mused, my pen has produced that elusive best seller but my publishers have forgotten to tell me; the glossy brochure enclosed showed a magnificent automobile – alongside a price displaying seemingly more noughts than in the National Debt.

Also, there was a neat letter inviting me to drive the beast; truly, a moment to savour. Mind you, except for the diamond earrings, perhaps there are similarities between Lewis Hamilton and myself! The offer, though, enticing though it is, will not be taken up. Were I to be tempted, Ann and the family would invoke the pre-paid funeral plan; anyway, this exotic machine would never fit in our garage. Still, if this is an example of future 'junk mail', then let it flow.

I gazed in astonishment – perhaps, at last, I mused, my pen has produced that elusive best seller but my publishers have forgotten to tell me!

11

It's a Generation Thing

*T*HERE are numerous phrases and sayings invoked when describing human nature, behaviour and attitudes plus differences regarding the way folk act and live. Some are trite, others sensible, a few, profound. Amongst this third grouping is, one feels, a four word observation which cuts to the heart of the way people prioritise matters – indeed, view the world: 'It's a generation thing'.

During those moments of repose contemplating the universe of today and the one I knew in my youth, it occurs to me that my outlook, habits and beliefs are often very different from those of my sons – and even more divergent from that of my grandchildren.

Here, of course, I talk personally – I have no right to assume I speak for others. Observation, though, encourages me to believe that my attitudes and approach to life are not so very different to those of numerous contemporaries. For so many of us pensioners were brought up to believe in 'The Protestant work ethic' – another four word phrase of immense influence back then. Assuredly it is deeply ingrained in myself; I have made some foolish decisions during my life work-wise but I have always done just that – worked.

The earning of a living, naturally, has been a prime mover but it goes beyond this; for my upbringing, that of my wife, Ann, plus so many of our generation, was based upon the premise that reward came only from effort and labour; not to work, unless unavoidable, was a sin, whilst leisure, like money, had to be earned. Even now, though semi-retired, we both tend to feel ill at ease – if not guilty – if we sit down and relax during the daytime. To do so on a Sunday is permissible – that's the 'official' day of rest; any other time, however, is a different matter.

Should we be resting when weeds could well be poking their ugly heads through the soil in our garden; when possibly the windows could do with a clean; when the car needs a wash, the bedrooms a hoovering? Yes, of course we should. We've earned it and deep down we know we have; yet the unease still lingers.

To a degree, it's the same when on holidays. There is a sun drenched, golden sanded beach to lie upon, a lagoon-like pool to lounge beside, glass in hand – and most folk under 60 will be doing just that. Some of us of more mature years, though, are just as likely to go on a 10-mile 'yomp' across hostile terrain, return exhausted, then declaim to a largely uncomprehending audience, 'Well, we've earned our lunch!' How daft is this; we are on a holiday which assuredly we deserve, along with a proliferation of lunches. The vast majority of younger people whilst, on the whole, hard working, reliable and disciplined, do not feel guilt about taking leisure or holidays, or relaxing in general – nor should they.

Mind you, there are fields in which less aged generations

might benefit, I feel, if they sought to emulate their parents and grandparents. Respect is a major area. There is often a marked lack of this shown by younger people to those of advanced years; not that there should be necessarily deference but there could be an acknowledgement that age brings more than stiffness, running noses and the like; with it, often, comes experience of life, understanding of human nature, judgement, common sense – at times, even wisdom. Also, older folk often have greater regard for the law, for the rights of others, even, perhaps – in a sense – the environment as they will probably drop less litter and the like. Certainly they would seem to have greater devotion to democracy, in that they are far more likely to vote in elections. There can be little that is more disrespectful to those who, over the decades, have fought and died for freedom, than the cavalier spurning of the ballot box by many in their prime.

However, from a male perspective, amongst the greatest divergences between the generations lies in the raising of children. In a previous article I afflicted patient readers with a diatribe concerning 'modern fathers'; I'll not repeat it except to say I have respect, even admiration, for the 'hands on' involvement of numerous young fellows in the rearing of their children – vastly greater than my own and probably the bulk of my age group.

The flip side of the coin, though, is that there are far more single mothers, in the present era, left to bring up children, with young husbands or partners shirking responsibilities in terms of both care and finance.

So there you go – 'swings and roundabouts'. A fair bet, though, is that in 50 years time an elderly generation will bemoan the failings of the modern.

12

Job Adverts

*B*EING a man who both enjoys his work and, in order to maintain a reasonable standard of living, has appreciation of the 'pennies' which come in payment, I am ever mindful that in this tough and, often, unfair world, nothing is certain.

Thus that I am a touch nervous that one day I could be called into the office and be told 'Sorry, but we are going to have to let you go' – which always seems to be a daft phrase as it suggests one is being held a prisoner; I certainly do not wish to be released from my 'bondage'. If such a calamity did befall – and it has in the past, more than once – I would, of course, look for another job; finding one, though, would be a very different matter – potential employers would not be casting covetous eyes in my direction.

Firstly, there is my age – indeed, the 'Grim Reaper' could well arrive at my door before the P45. Then there is the matter of skills and flair – I possess little of either; granted I have, despite this, managed always to find employment during my long, very varied working life but mastery of the arcane sciences that are IT and technology in general, has become ever more crucial – all of it well beyond me. Still, there are jobs which, I feel, I still retain sufficient energy, experience and basic common sense to do. Perusing employment adverts (I do so regularly to 'keep my hand in') fills me with apprehension, however – even alarm. The great majority, of course, require acumen which I do not possess – and never will; such are discarded, instantly.

It is, though, with the small number which, in terms of ability, come within my scope the problem lies; for so many of such ads nowadays would appear to require not only 'aptitude' but 'attitude'. Memory suggests perhaps inaccurately – as mine is an aged brain – that in the not too distant past, potential employers would lay down the competences they required from applicants, possibly state salary on offer (though in this, so often, low pay area, that might well be avoided), then await approaches.

Now, though, in so many recruitment blurbs, requirements go well beyond this; for instance, a restaurateur needing waiting personnel might state as being essential, not the, to me, important quality that they be efficient – rather, they be 'enthusiastic'. Now the dictionary describes this word as 'exceptional zeal'; is this what a diner wants when enjoying a leisurely meal, a steward buzzing about like a demented bee?

In some jobs such a stated requirement would alarm – imagine the panic amongst car owners if local authorities advertised for 'enthusiastic' traffic wardens. Then there is stated by many seeking staff in varying occupations, the demand that those applying be 'dedicated'. Chambers here describes the word as meaning 'to set apart and consecrate to some sacred purpose; to devote wholly or chiefly'. One fears that the stability of most folk's married and family lives would be put in jeopardy should their employment require such all consuming devotion.

Another term which pops up with some regularity, the exhortation that anyone seeking the position advertised should be 'committed'; this one, in reality, is pointless – even senseless. Do not employees (in theory, at least) automatically commit themselves to their tasks the moment they enter their place of work? Some potential hirers wish applicants to be 'keen'; recently one desired such a mindset from a general farm worker whose tasks would include early morning milking. It would be, indeed, a singular person who would view rising at 5am, then going out to bring in the herd on a black winter's morning, in foul weather, with buoyant relish. The crucial aspect would be that they could be relied upon to do so – not that they enjoyed it.

Then there is the most overused and, arguably, abused, term of all; catering establishments seem no longer to seek the services of men and women merely of a culinary bent – no, they require chefs 'passionate' about food; recently a nursing home advertised for assistants, likewise, regarding caring for the elderly. Possibly that which could win gold, if there was an Olympic competition for absurd use of this evocative word, was in an entry from estate agents wishing to bring on board a person 'passionate about letting'; words fail me – well, almost, I can still muster a few more, just.

These are to suggest – respectfully, for quite rightly 'he

who pays the piper, calls the tune' – that such adjectives are meaningless lather. A worker owes an employer effort, skills, reliability, honesty, courtesy and loyalty; the boss should reciprocate loyalty and courtesy, and add respect, security, decent pay and conditions, plus trust. Let's ditch the froth – it's the beer which counts.

13

No Problem!

A WHILE back, feeling a touch peckish, I went into a local bakery to purchase what has to be – next to the cream tea – Devon and Cornwall's finest creation.

'A pasty, please,' said I to the youngish gent behind the counter. His reply was both affable and positive – but, frankly, trite.

'No problem,' said he.

Well, seeing as the sign outside the shop stated, in letters some six inches high, the alluring solitary word, 'Pasties', I never thought there would be; such confidence had been reinforced upon entry by the sight of trays of the succulent pastry encased delights in sufficient numbers to assuage the hunger of a regiment of soldiers. I found it was a creation to be proud of and it was much enjoyed; thus, a few days later, was back for another. This time, following my request, he smiled in friendly fashion, said 'No worries', then presented me with my lunch.

Again, a little later in the day, I considered his gently spoken words as I devoured his very satisfactory product; of course there were 'no worries', I mused. Once again he was surrounded by a multitude of the meat and potato parcels, but even if he hadn't been – even if he had just supplied that regiment and was sold out – it was not something to worry about; the state of the nation and that of Plymouth Argyle – such are the directions in which concerns should be directed.

Regarding my meal, if he had not been able to supply it, there were half a dozen other establishments no great distance away which could – and would – with alacrity; assuredly it was never anything I was going to fret over. Still, the gent involved here was ever pleasant with a welcoming demeanour, whilst his fast foods were first class; so I patronised, regularly, his establishment. Sadly, I am no longer able to; he has moved to another town where he now owns a far larger bakery. Thus clearly the quality of his product endeared him to an ever increasing legion of customers, as should be the case – and which puts my petty nitpicking into perspective; still, serial old moaner that I am, I do feel the need to scatter a few more gripes regarding the use of repetitive, tired phrases.

There is a small, local store where one is served by a most charming lady, perpetually appearing to be in a happy mood. Her words of greeting, though, have a remarkable consistency; to be fair, the opening pair do vary a little; she will always say, initially, 'Morning,' (no matter what time of the day), but the word following varies – it can be 'love', 'dear', 'darling', even 'sweetheart'. This, though, will be followed with 'Same old weather' – words expressed in an area where the elements are about as reliable as a baby's bowels, where its capriciousness will usually be a topic amongst her customers. If only she would state a tolerably accurate appraisal of the climactic conditions to be found outside her shop; granted a trivial matter and not one really worth complaining about, but it is often the minutiae of life which irk most.

Then there is a fellow I've known for many a long year whom often I see about town, and whenever I do he invariably greets me with 'All right, boy? Not many, of us left.' Seeing as the population of these islands and, indeed, the world, is growing by an alarming rate, this is a statement of extraordinary inaccuracy.

Another gentleman will usually greet one with a somewhat despairing shake of the head, followed by the rather apocalyptic prophesy, 'Glad I'm not born now; we've had the best of it.' One feels he would say the same no matter if the future for one and all appeared glorious. Mind you, despite this, in his eyes, sad deterioration of the world about him, it's most doubtful he is in any hurry to leave it. There are, of course, so many more words, phrases, cliches, uttered by men and women alike which are platitudinous, tired, obvious, foolish, exasperating, vexing, even plain daft.

Is it not perhaps a touch sad that though arguably possessors of the richest, most expressive, assuredly most used language on earth, often we British employ such little originality and imagination in its use?

Having said all this, however, it is time for a personal confession; I am the user of a limited, but I suspect, rather annoying number of set, inane utterances, which I invoke with mindless regularity. They tend to leave my lips before my brain has even begun to engage and often are imbued with words of excruciating banality; thus this article is penned by a hypocrite!

14

Passion – & Pasties

WHILST, to my mind, it ended on a slightly discordant note, such was related to food rather than football. As will be remembered, in January Plymouth Argyle were involved in one of the most important and high profile FA Cup ties to come their way in a generation.

Battling through to round three – thanks to a brace of away victories – they were sentenced to travel again (and in professional football there are no short journeys for the Pilgrims or, of course, their magnificent, loyal, numerous safari-minded supporters, the 'Green Army'). On that January Sunday, however, fans relished the prospect of a 300 mile (or thereabouts) expedition across winter terrain to the north west of England to do battle with one of the elite sides in world football, Liverpool.

More than 9,000 made the pilgrimage to Anfield and at least a similar number of green garbed followers would have done so if they'd been able to obtain tickets. Those who did traverse most of England were well rewarded; for Argyle, thanks to a rearguard performance of valiance and discipline, invoking the 'Dunkirk spirit', held the famed

Reds to a goalless draw; thus – a replay at Home Park.

Suddenly, 'regular' supporters of the Pilgrims exploded in number from around 10,000 per game (cold statistics state) to three times the number. Folk who'd, perhaps, been to Home Park no more than a handful of times since the splitting of the atom classed the stadium as their second home and badgered the club for tickets. Though little fault could be attached to Argyle, mayhem threatened (computer 'gremlins' did not help), but was avoided – just – with most genuine fans getting the coveted entry pass. Not all were fortunate, however; unfairly, some who needed a sat-nav to locate the ground got their hands on them.

The game itself was one to savour – emerald clad 'Davids' in titanic combat with crimson garbed 'Goliaths'. Sadly, the outcome was the reverse of the biblical result, the Lancastrian giants (and millionaires) scoring the only goal of the game – indeed, of the two matches.

So the Reds moved into the next round while the Plymouth club was left (that most hackneyed of football phrases) to 'concentrate on the league'. For once, though, such words have relevance; clearly the Pilgrims were never going to win the cup, but they do, at last, have a realistic prospect of bringing an end to six consecutive campaigns in the dark depths of football's fourth tier. Into this they fell following back-to-back relegations, in 2010 and 2011, from the second level; thus there has been virtually a decade of debilitating failure, including chronic financial ills which almost sent this famous old club into oblivion.

Argyle, at present, however, are right up there at the promotion end of the league table; also, the cup run has revitalised interest among many previously jaded supporters and, crucially, has put more than a million pounds into their bank.

Following the final whistle that replay night, there was a presentation in the club's boardroom which, on the part of the hosts, was thoughtful and imaginative.

At the end of the Anfield tie, Liverpool's German manager, Jurgen Klopp – clearly unhappy to face a further fixture – enquired: 'How far is it to Plymouth?' His answer came via an unusual gift courtesy of the well-known baking company which sponsors the Greens. A magnificent pasty, its size and weight ensuring it required two sturdy fellows to do the bearing, was presented to the visiting boss; carved upon it the data: 'Liverpool to Plymouth, 293 miles'. He accepted it with thanks, then asked what it was. When told, it is reported he said, a touch ungraciously, that he could not eat it as it was full of carbohydrates!

Really? I must say this puzzles me, for having devoured 'oggies' since I was weaned, I've always found them to contain the likes of meat, turnip, onions and spuds, with the casing being tasty pastry – a magnificent creation, arguably the finest culinary delight ever to come out of Devon and Cornwall.

These days, mind you, a range of tastes are catered for: cheese and onion, chicken, even curry-flavoured fillings proving popular. Herr Klopp, it appears, sees this sustaining dish as being unhealthy; this is hard to take from a member of the race that eats fatty sausages the size of rolling pins, rich, cream-laden gateaux and drinks beer from beakers the size of buckets. It is to be hoped that if he did not value this mammoth feast, he passed it on to someone who would; perhaps the Anfield faithful – there's plenty of them and they need cheering up at present.

15

Christmas

*L*IKE Tavistock Goose Fair, it comes but once a year; some folk though, lament the fact that it's every year – and is almost upon us again.

Just a few days ago, a lady astonished me when she remarked that she felt it had 'crept up on us' – so 'quiet' things had been, she could scarce believe it was as close. Now it is hard to fathom her opinion that the looming Yuletide has adopted a stealthy approach; for has it not – as is usual – hurtled our way with all the subtle lightness of foot of an obese leviathan? Since late summer shops have been bedecked with tinsel and decorations, shelves groaning with potential presents, plus seasonal greetings cards which are inclusive, virtually, of all possible members of a household – probably even including the hamster. Supermarkets have been awash with a tidal wave of goodies guaranteed to suit all but the most pernickety of tastes – meat, poultry, a vast array of savouries ranging from the traditional to the exotic; and for those with sweet teeth (being one myself, sadly I have few left), a divine panoply of confection the like of which might well be seen – and

Christmas just crept up on her!

drooled over – on the *Great British Bake Off*, plus mountains of chocolate and lagoons of liquor.

Newspapers, local and national, have bulged with advertising hammering home to hapless, ever more stressed potential buyers the threat that Christmas and the New Year are approaching with all the gentle decorum of a herd of demented buffaloes. A multitude from hotels, restaurants, cafes, pubs and the like are extolling the virtues of their, generally, traditional menus (so many sourced from 'locally grown produce') leading up to December 25 – many on that day as well.

A majority emblazon their adverts with an exhortation – prospective diners should 'book early to avoid disappointment'; in the words of John McEnroe – 'You cannot be serious'. For here we have in our area (and almost certainly in every district in the land) multiple establishments from hostelries to church halls, providing seasonal meals both during the day and evenings for weeks – indeed months – on end. In total there could be, in the run-up to December 25, sufficient meals to feed, for a day or two at least, a goodly portion of the population of China. Clearly their clientele booking early (just booking, in fact) will aid those providing the food – amount to order, to prepare, to cook and so forth – and lead, hopefully, to a shorter period for diners having to await their fare; but chances of there being 'no room at the inn' (especially the dining area) surely are remote.

Prominent also in our vibrant local papers are stylish supplements encouraging young and old alike to forsake their cosy abodes and turn out for an abundance of fun, treats and bargains to be found – bolstered by a merry atmosphere – in many streets in our West Devon towns on late shopping-evenings.

Nothing wrong with this, mind you, but this 'miserable toad' of a scribe perpetually objects to what is, in my jaundiced opinion, the highly inappropriate – surely hypocritical – titles given them. For there is a 'Victorian' evening, an 'Edwardian' event and, of course, the annual 'Dickensian', all held locally during November and early December. These usually are successful events (though dependent to an extent on weather) with traders and shopkeepers experiencing decent sales, whilst many folk find these evenings both enjoyable and useful in terms of sociability and the buying of festive presents.

The minus to me, however, is the maudlin sentimentality which abounds in the eulogising of 19th century Yuletides; for the reality is that for so many people throughout this land, there was scant joy; millions were blighted by poverty; and the celebration of Christmas brought little relief. By all means remember the way of life in the Victorian era – but give thanks that here in the 21st century our lives, generally, are free of privation and exploitation – as are our celebrations.

Still, whatever our feelings and outlook regarding the upcoming, to some, jollities, to others upheavals, they are not, assuredly, slinking up on us despite the notions of the lady who has been unaware of it all happening around her. The lookout on the *Titanic*, who did not have a good day – and whose lack of perception was infinitely more calamitous – could not have been less observant. No, it's coming all right, like a meteorite; in fact it's almost here. Even the church seems to be trying to get in on it these days. Is nothing sacred?

Whatever – it'll be magical when it comes; have a great time – a happy fulfilling Christmas to one and all.

16

The Shipping Forecast

THOUGH a proud native of one of the world's greatest nautical nations, and despite being born and bred in the county of Drake, assuredly I am no sailor; in fact, I can't even swim.

I much prefer to fly over the seas than plough their waves when travelling to distant lands. This is down partially to my curse of suffering from chronic impatience (one moves somewhat faster in the air than on the water), but also due to my constitution being more sturdy aloft than on undulating liquid. However, I would still claim, for a 'landlubber', at least a modicum of awareness of seafaring matters; not so much as how to sail a yacht, or handle boat or ship I hasten to add – I would probably be even worse at that than DIY (truly the depths of personal ineptitude) – but rather on the meteorological front.

When it comes to 'sailing the seven seas', weather has probably greater relevance than all else and here I do have a grasp – albeit small – of the turbulent nature of the waters within tolerable proximity of our islands.

Mind you, Ann has a much greater knowledge of, and

love for, seafaring matters than do I; as a girl she lived for a while in Padstow and on occasions went out on fishing vessels and the small working boats that made the regular rounds of checking lobster pots and the like for their potential harvest. She certainly retains an interest in nautical issues; like myself, most mornings she lies abed listening to the shipping forecast, broadcast daily at 5.20am on BBC Radio 4.

For a relatively modest sized land area, there are a surprisingly high number of sea areas adjoining, or in proximity to, the United Kingdom. There is 'Dogger', long time prime location for trawlers and 'Fisher', which sounds as if it should be; also the exotically named 'North' and 'South Utsire' which have, one feels, titles more suitable to the oceans beyond South America than the North Sea.

Then there is the slightly sinister sounding 'German Bight', and the mildly alarming 'Viking'; it is to be hoped folk from the latter now follow respectable employment and have ceased ambitions to cross icy waters to pursue a somewhat anti-social pillaging.

The small island of 'Lundy', off the coast of North Devon, has a sizeable zone named after it, as does 'Rockall', a lump of granite in the Irish Sea. Surprisingly, in such a large number of areas, only one is named after a city – 'Plymouth'; immediately this makes one suspect that we who live reasonably close to the 'Ocean City' (as it is described) are possibly more vulnerable to the, at times, turbulent British weather than most others. The forecast for sailors, mind you, is but the first of a trilogy of prophesies regarding the seas which the Met Office broadcasts at this early hour, for it is followed immediately by 'reports from coastal stations' – statistics provided by climatic installations sited around our long, meandering seaboard. One is informed if that faithful harbinger of weather, the barometer, is rising or falling, along with other information of a technical nature.

Helpful to the non sailor who might just be considering a visit to the beach, is the last of the three forecasts for 'inshore waters'; here listeners are informed of climatic prospects for at least 24 hours around the country's perimeter; sun, rain, fogs, frost, wind speeds and the like. By the time the lady or gent from the Met Office has delivered this mountain of information, they must feel like taking the rest of the day off. Mind you, often our surfeit, Ann and I, of this nautical intelligence will not be the initial radio experience of the day; on occasions it will have been preceded by a plethora of news provided by the excellent BBC World Service.

We will have been apprised of such events as anarchy in Azerbaijan, blood baths in Borneo, calamity in Cambodia, drought in Djibouti, massacres in Mali, pestilence in Panama, revolution in Rwanda, tsunamis in Thailand and the like – if really fortunate, we will be given some good news from some obscure spot on the globe.

Now anybody reading this might well ask why we pass many night hours listening to radio when we should be slumbering; fair point; but that is the problem – so often we cannot sleep! Insomnia's cruel grip gets ever tighter. Whilst it can be instructive to know what's happening at sea and interesting to be informed of world events, the place we would most like to visit is 'the Land of Nod'.

17

Prejudices & Jargon

WHILST I must admit to harbouring prejudice, I rarely get too upset over what people do – as long as it is within the law and (a selfish attitude) does not affect me adversely.

What folk say though – hackneyed phrases, banal asides, platitudes and the like – well that is a different matter.

In my, admittedly, jaundiced view, few add to the appraisal of a situation, understanding of the world or human nature – indeed, contribute much in any way that is meaningful; some in fact are, when analysed, mindless. For example, you might hear of a calamity; could be a terrorist attack, a multiple pile up on a motorway, a tsunami destroying life, or on a local level, the untimely tragic demise of someone well known in the local community. Such news is passed onto a friend, acquaintance or colleague; they gaze at you in, understandably, shocked fashion then utter the words, 'you're joking'! Can there be any response more fatuous? After all, it would be the most twisted of minds that could create such catastrophe in pursuit of jest.

There is a further response that invokes my impotent ire; there you are having a really bad day, perhaps the car has broken down, a gale has blown slates off the roof of your house or the P45 has just arrived in the post along with the bill for the previous time the auto caused problems. In depressed despair, this rash of misfortune is mentioned to another; their response? At times one of sympathy, but it is not rare to be confronted with the crass 'tell me about it.' An obvious retort would be simply to say 'I just have.' However, their idiotic comment is usually a way of implying that no matter what has befallen you, it is trivial compared to the burdens they have to bear. Similarly there are those who, when events are not to their liking, state self-pityingly – 'just my luck,' as if it is solely them who endure misfortune.

Mind you, it is not just negativity which stirs my wrath – some positivity can also. An example (to me at least) is when one comments to somebody on a freezing, albeit bright, winter's day, the wind from Siberia, 'bitter weather;' and often the reaction; 'yes – nice though.' How daft is this; it's almost cold enough to freeze blood in the veins, yet it is deemed acceptable simply because it isn't raining. If precipitation is required to alleviate temperature (as it often is in winter), then bring it on – please.

Now, whilst probably only a minority will share my disgruntlement over the gripes I've penned up to now, I suspect they could be more in sympathy with my antagonism towards 'jargon'. The Oxford reference dictionary describes this as being 'debased language/gibberish'. To be fair, it has probably always polluted our great mother tongue, but not to the degree it does today. This is due, possibly, to American influence, plus, perhaps, social media. It affects the younger generation more savagely than those of mature years though longevity does not guarantee immunity. Sadly it seems to be employed exhaustively by ambitious young people in the world of banking, business, commerce and such-like – men and women with, one might hope, sufficient acumen and education to be able to mobilize our comprehensive, rich tongue with some originality, insight and relevance.

The reality, however, is that some executive, absurdly juvenile, will exhort colleagues, asinine words flowing from their lips like lava from Vesuvius, to 'hit the ground running,' employ 'blue sky thinking,' work or be available '24/7', ensure opposition is confronted on a 'level playing field,' aid the cause by ensuring their 'ducks are in a row'; always they must be prepared for 'dialogue', to 'emphasise the positive, eliminate the negative' and should matters really go awry, be prepared to 'think the unthinkable'. After such pep talks, often the next stage is a 'bonding' session – employees often coerced into wasting their time indulging in pointless group activities which, in reality, might create disunity and ill-will as opposed to bringing colleagues together.

The 'B' word one feels, has so much to answer for – not least when it comes to modern parenting; for it appears it is deemed essential in these times that mothers and fathers make strenuous – often synthetic – efforts to 'bond' with their offspring. Such strong ties, of course, are of the highest value, but will not the vast majority of mums who carry a child for nine often difficult months have those automatically, as will most proud dads, also. So is there the need to put aside 'quality time' (as opposed, one assumes, to 'rubbish time') towards the entertaining and upbringing of 'junior'? Surely a child needs but two constants from parents, security and love – especially the latter.

18

Age Never Comes Alone

*E*VEN if one's health is basically sound (fortunately, mine is), 'Age never comes alone' – as the saying goes; the body and brain respond to instructions in ever more sluggish fashion. A cause of this could be the fact (apparently) that in the average human, even before one's 30th birthday, brain cells are dying at a faster rate than they are being replaced. I suspect mine are down to single figures, rattling in lonely, aimless fashion around an ancient cranium; the chilling awareness is that they will get fewer.

The rate and extent of the deterioration of mental capacity varies greatly; some favoured folk can make old age with relatively little decline of faculties, but they are probably a minority. Also, it is not just the slowing of the thought processes (though such are perhaps most crucial) that signpost the rocky, ever more fraught journey leading towards longevity – though some are clearly far less afflicted by decay than others, they being burdened by little more than, say, a slight slowing of pace, a minor thickening of waist, a greying of hair; mind you, such has not been a problem regarding my own follicles, a large percentage forsaking my pate during my thirties well before amendment to colour is anticipated.

It is said that baldness, often, is inherited; not true in my case, for not a solitary member of either my father's or mother's families had lost hair to any extent, even in old age. What caused it, I know not; sadly it has not been down to an excessively dissipated way of life – it could though, in part, be down to a lifetime of following Plymouth Argyle. Still it is not something to lie awake worrying about – assuredly not like the value of the pound, the state of the nation or the chances of the team winning promotion, at last.

Something which, until the past few years, worried me not was the state of my teeth. The occasional one fell out, now and again a humane dentist would do an extraction (at enormous expense) but I never worried as there always appeared to be an ample number remaining. Then, not long ago, 1 realised that even my brain cells were more abundant than my 'gnashers'; in consequence, my few remaining molars have been in intensive care, and I've spent, seemingly, more time in a dentist's chair than at work. Dentures, also, have come my way – useful as long as one does not try to bite on anything firmer than a blancmange. Eschewing the munching of pork scratchings is no hardship – abstaining from the devouring of toffees, however, assuredly is. Being a man who relishes his food, having to judge the hardness of all I really enjoy is a strain; mind you, one bit of advice from my dentist I always ignore is his suggestion that I avoid eating all things sweet. To fall in line with this would be, to me, an abandonment of one of the true joys of life.

Another area from which I derive pleasure is reading and writing; now, whilst I may have increasing problems with this in terms of acumen and concentration, the actual scanning holds no fears as my 'short sight' remains quite good; distance, though, is a very different matter. Until the age of 50, or so, I had never experienced any trouble when it came to my eyes; about that time, however, increasingly I realised that my ability to view, accurately, people or objects just a modest distance away was deteriorating – I could have made a real life cameo appearance in one of those adverts concerning ocular deficiencies stating where 'they should have gone.'

So before the age of 60 I was well into the grip of the ageing process; it has tightened. The legs are getting stiffer, whilst the back is an issue especially when I try to raise it from the mattress of a morning. I'm not especially worried in this direction, however. It is mainly with the senses, that trouble lies – as is the case with so many of us of mature years. It was pinpointed recently when visited by one of our sons; he said he could hear our television as he was approaching the house; to me it was barely loud enough. An audience with the audiologist ensued; surprisingly, this young gent felt that a hearing aid was not required imminently, but that the situation could alter – sooner rather than later.

As to the TV – 'use the subtitles' said he; we do, but the technology betrays us – the words, inexorably, appear to diminish in size. Still, to finish on a positive note, the taste buds remain sound; chocolate and whisky still bring pleasure to life.

19

The Wing Nut

*T*O be fair, it was not a calamity which would register high on the 'Richter scale' of disaster; more of an annoyance – one of those trivial malfunctions which can affect even the most efficiently run households, which, thanks to my remarkably calm, able wife, Ann, ours is.

We had family staying for a few days, and had greatly enjoyed their company. Just before they left, however, it was reported that there was something amiss with the toilet seat in the bathroom. On checking, it was clear this was no exaggeration, for it was swivelling around like the 'waltzers' in a fairground. It would have been beneficial to have been able to call upon the services of someone of sound common sense, practical ability plus the tools and parts needed to put matters right.

Ann was able to provide the first three requirements, but her accurate diagnosis of the defect could not lead to a cure without the necessary intact spare. The acquisition of this seemed to pose few problems and minimal expense; the fault appeared to be very simple – one of the two bolts which held the seat in place had been dislodged, this due to the fact that the wing nut which held it in place had fractured and dropped off. The disintegration of the crucial locking device was not a major surprise, for it had about as much substance as a cobweb, being a flimsy piece of plastic; even to my mind – one illiterate in practical matters – it looked totally inadequate for the purpose for which it was created, that of keeping a heavy, sturdy seat in place. Whatever – it needed replacing.

Thus a trip to town to a hardware store; 'they're bound to have one,' said I to Ann, with some confidence; misplaced. Entering the large shop, I went to the counter where I was confronted in friendly fashion by a courteous young fellow. I placed the battered piece of white plastic in front of him and then requested a replacement – 'two, in fact,' said I, aware that the insubstantial screw could well succumb to wear and tear rapidly.

The salesman picked it up, then inspected it with an intensity which could not be surpassed by an archeologist gazing at a rare artefact. There was a blowing out of cheeks, a scratching, then shaking of the head – 'Don't think we've anything like this,' said he. 'What's it used for?'

A synopsis of its purpose was given; a colleague was summoned. The young gent explained to his older workmate the situation; there following a similar blowing, scratching and shaking.

'Got nothing like that I'm afraid; you best try. . .' the name of a local builders' merchant was mentioned. 'It's more their line than ours.'

Why a simple wing nut was not part of the stock of a shop dedicated to DIY was something I could not be bothered to enquire. I left the store and hurtled to the suggested premises (no time to waste – a lavatory is amongst the most essential and frequently used facilities of any home). Progress was being made – the lady at the counter was immediately aware of the function which the battered bit of plastic performed. She also agreed with me that it was clearly not substantial enough. She then became afflicted with the head shaking syndrome – 'Sorry, it's not the sort of thing we stock on its own; we've only got it as part of the fixing kit which comes with the seats. You'll need to buy the whole thing I'm afraid – though I can probably give you 10 per cent off.'

I thanked her, then left the building with alacrity; spend a sum of money sufficient to buy a decent bottle of single malt? Not likely. There was a similar emporium close by so I tried my luck a third time. Again the news that the miniscule, but vital part I required only came with the seat itself.

A helpful chap, he came back with an idea. 'Out the back we've some old seats that are damaged; it could be there's a nut like this on one of them.'

Off he went, returning five minutes later clutching a precious plastic wing nut. Joy abounded – prematurely; it was the wrong size. We shared a session of synchronised head shaking; positivity, though, returned.

'Why don't you try the market? There's a stall that sells this type of thing.'

Thanking him, I sallied forth to this 'Aladdin's Cave'; the owner seeing what was required, delved into a battered tray holding multitudes of assorted screws, nuts, bolts and such-like, soon producing an aged metal wing nut.

'Try this.'

I did just that; it fitted perfectly.

Cost? Twenty pence; I can afford the whisky after all.

20

Desert Island Discs

*B*EING an occasional listener to *Desert Island Discs* running, remarkably, since the end of the Second World War, I sometimes muse over the recordings I might choose; mind you, whilst my vulnerability to being cast away on a desert island is minimal, the likelihood of being invited onto the airwaves to be interviewed by the charming Kirsty Young, is nil.

Yet such reflections can, in a trivial but mildly interesting way, divert the mind from wrestling with vexatious every day issues and problems. For instance, the castaway has to name a book he or she would wish to have (the Bible and the complete works of Shakespeare are supplied automatically); tough this, but probably I would take Heinrich Harrer's fascinating *Seven Years in Tibet*, an evocative narrative of the Austrian's life, in the 1940s, in this almost medieval land on 'the roof of the world'.

As to a luxury, my taste buds dominate; for I would love them to be caressed, very regularly, with ample draughts of whisky and wine plus calorie laden dollops of the finest chocolates. If I'm to be on this island for a long time then

d

*My luxury – ample draughts of whisky and wine
plus calorie laden dollops of the finest chocolates.*

stocks of such would need to be comprehensive; the inevitable heat would necessitate the availability of a large refrigerated cave to accommodate it. Sadly, I feel these luxuries would not be within the rules.

Still, the recordings are what the programme, mainly, is about – the eight which might bring solace to the lonely listener in their sun-drenched prison. I am not musical; I can play no instrument, can't sing and am unable to read it, yet, as a listener, it brings me pleasure, with my tastes being quite eclectic. To choose the limited number of discs the rules require would be hard – but here goes!

Frank Sinatra has to be included; indeed if permitted, I would take the longest of extended albums of the unique sound of 'Ole Blue Eyes', but if restricted to a solitary single, then possibly, *Strangers in the Night* (though tomorrow I might well choose something else). Another of my favourites is 'The Little Sparrow' – Edith Piaf. Physically tiny, she possessed a voice remarkable in terms of decibels and, like Sinatra, it was in a class of its own; her *No Regrets* would be a firm choice – and sung in her native tongue, as in French, though I scarcely understand a word, that vibrant, piercing sound has even greater resonance. Luciano Pavarotti, also, has to be there; that tenor larynx hitting the top note of *Nessun Dorma* is sublime. The gritty realism of Country and Western has attraction for me; Johnny Cash's unique tone has much appeal but Kenny Rogers is the singer of the number I'll be listening to on that sandy shore. He articulates well – one can hear every word he warbles which, to me, is important, as I like to absorb the lyrics as well as music. In *The Gambler* his lines such as 'Know when to walk away, know when to run', can, at times, be a shrewd guide to the living of life. A profound observation of the world, and those dwelling in it sometimes less fortunate, comes from my favourite Beatles' effort, *Eleanor Rigby*; poignantly, at the funeral of this solitary lady, nobody came – a chilling thought provoking observation in what would definitely be included in my eight.

Amongst them too would be that stirring John Philip Sousa march, *Semper Fidelis*; rousing in its own right, to we Plymouth Argyle supporters it has an emotional pull, it being the blast of brass with which the team, for generations, has taken to the pitch. There could, as well, be a bonus in listening to it on the island, as I might feel the trauma of life in this faraway spot is still less than that to be found at Home Park and thus be content to remain there.

Whilst rhythm is important, I have always loved the spoken word. It would be tempting to take some of the wartime speeches of Winston Churchill, but, here I am going to be (to my shame) a touch unpatriotic. For what better way to mitigate, to a degree, the solitude of this desolate place, than to hear the powerful, rousing, lyrical, rich tones of Martin Luther King saying he has 'A dream today'; there are those who class this as, possibly, the most memorable speech ever – I'd not argue with that.

So, only one slot remaining to be filled – but a multitude of recordings to choose from. Again I am going to eschew harmony and go for prose – the sumptuous Welsh voice of Richard Burton reading from *Under Milk Wood*, the masterpiece of his countryman, Dylan Thomas.

These then are my eight. The problem? – simply to hear each I'll have to buy them, for I will never have access to the vast BBC archives.

21

The Christening

*N*EVER much good at making decisions – well, the right ones, that is – I delegated it to Ann.

The shirt and suit were no problem – they were ideal for manifold official occasions, especially in church. The problem, though, was that the black tie – used so often these days it is hung up with the car keys – was not appropriate; assuredly not. For the afternoon was to be spent, firstly in church, then in a nearby hall, celebrating the arrival of someone into the world not their departure.

Attendance at weddings these days is a rare event, whilst Christenings come along about as often as an Argyle promotion season. Such a welcome of new life was to take place in the parish church on a glorious Sunday afternoon, and for Ann and I it was special – the naming of our first great-grandchild. Granted, such senior status in a family inevitably is accompanied by advancing years, but personally I relish it; being the youngest of three sons – and so often in my youth being referred to as the 'baby of the family' – it is strangely satisfying to be the oldest of our immediate tribe; to have reached an age when no matter how eccentric one's behaviour, or cynical one's views (well, within reason, that is), those around you generally grit their teeth and accept it (though often with pained expressions and a rolling of eyes, gestures which suggest that internally they are saying, 'the old fool's at it again').

So we set off for the parish church, on that blistering day, full of bonhomie and good will to all; Ann, as always, looked lovely, whilst I sported the richly hued tie she had chosen for me after much deliberation. Was it worth the effort? Personally, being a man of tradition and convention, I feel it was as it acknowledged not just a happy occasion, but a significant one – an important milestone (after birth, the earliest) on the, hopefully, long road leading through a full life. In my judgement, formality was required; also attired in such neckwear was my brother Stan – a gent, of course, of similar vintage and views on sartorial etiquette. We were alone in such dress – just as we were age-wise.

There was a far more unified approach amongst the ladies, mind you; irrespective of their longevity, virtually all were dressed in brightly hued summer finery – a delightful sight to even the most jaundiced eyes. The chaps, though were somewhat different; the request, apparently, had been to dress to a standard one was reasonably comfortable with, but at a minimum, 'smart casual'. The majority adhered to this, though there were a handful who appeared to pay more heed to the second word than the first.

The service started on time – crucial to this impatient old toad – and thanks to the warmth and positivity of the vicar, was an uplifting experience. *All Things Bright and Beautiful* was sung – a captivating hymn, but rather long on a hot day; then after prayers the half dozen prospective Godparents – three of each gender – all relatively young, were invited to make their promises regarding the spiritual and physical well being of Lily, the much loved daughter of Tom and Sammy. The vicar suggested all assembled spurn the ways of the Devil; this the gathering promised to do – earnestly. Then the church was traversed to the font for the act of baptism. With everyone clustered around, the vicar took the child in his arms then, dipping his fingers in water, made the sign of the cross on her forehead. For the first time, she reacted – a sizable wail coming from her lips. Someone commented, 'it's a sign of luck when they cry'; even to my addled old brain this did not sound the most profound prophesy in a soothsayer's repertoire; after all, who amongst us, of any age, if asleep would not react in anguished fashion to having a cup of cold water poured over our head.

The service over, the little girl officially named and back to her customary good humour – there was an explosion of 'paparazzi', seemingly more cameras clicking than at a film premiere. Lily took it all with aplomb, then was whisked across to a nearby hall for a most delectable – and filling – tea; the savouries were varied and satisfying, whilst to this scribe, the possessor of one of the 'sweetest teeth' in England, the desserts were divine.

Late afternoon saw this so very enjoyable and fulfilling occasion come to an end with most folk trundling home – though I fancy some of the younger folk might have gone for a ritual 'wetting of head'. I went home and placed the tie back in the rack; being a realist, though, I've left the black one with the car keys.

22

Appeasement

SIR Winston Churchill, ever the master of words, said that an appeaser was 'someone who fed a crocodile hoping it would eat them last.'

A man of perception with a shrewd understanding of human nature, it could be argued that nothing he ever said or wrote (and there is no shortage of either) was more telling or accurate than this. He, of course, was a robust, outspoken opponent of the flagrant, spineless conciliation towards the sabre rattlings of the increasingly bellicose Adolf Hitler during the mid and late 1930s. The aggression of this warlike German nation, its determination to bully – indeed, subsume states around it was clear to all but those who, at the time, simply did not wish to see, who had not the desire or will to confront a potentially vicious, ever more powerful, hostile race.

Sadly, the great bulk of European nations appeared to suffer from this self-induced myopia. However, history suggests that a tsunami of pacifism, allied to an almost criminal widespread ostrich-like 'burying of heads in the sand', gripped so-called statesmen throughout the Western democracies. Hitler and Deutschland – who could, and would, have been stopped in the mid 1930s if just a modicum of grit had been shown – devoured territories and enslaved people around their borders, gaining steadily in strength and confidence as those with the forces, and authority, to stop them did nothing. By the time the major military powers of Europe – notably Britain and France – decided a stand had to be made, it was too late to stop this Nazi juggernaut by any other means than to declare war against it. Thus followed the most destructive, pitiless conflict in history, with the 'crocodile' devouring so many of the states which had previously fed it.

Granted 'the beast' was destroyed eventually, but at what cost? Sadly, the stark realities of those dreadful times, and the lessons the free world should have learned from them, once more seem to be disregarded.

The atrocities committed by so-called Islamic State, by the Taliban, by the murderous regime of President Assad of Syria, leads to widespread 'hand wringing' throughout Europe; there is condemnation, talk of sanctions, murmurs of invoking international law and charging such murderers with genocide and the like; nothing, though, is actually done.

The bullies are not being confronted; and such is, essentially, what they are – thugs who impose their will and perverted beliefs, on others. In this, a dictator, terrorists, rampaging nations, are no different in a sense from a bully in the playground, or an abusive husband or father in the home; they have to be challenged – a stand has to be made. Such, of course, needs courage and plenty of it; it is worth remembering, though, that most of those who attempt to impose their will on others are generally cowards. When threatened with retaliation they will usually back off – especially if they feel they will be losers in conflict.

President Trump, when campaigning last year to be head of state of the world's most powerful nation, made few friends and accrued an even smaller number of admirers in the world at large. In the United States, however, (where it counted) he received sufficient votes to see him elected to the White House. Since taking office, his statements, actions and outlook have seemingly remained as mercurial, at times eccentric and often contradictory, as ever; even many of those who rightly respect the democratic will of the American people, and in consequence accept he must be given the benefit of the doubt, feel some unease over his policies and his, often, posturing.

Yet in at least one aspect of his foreign policy, is he not to be applauded? President Assad of Syria repeated an atrocity upon some of his own people that he had first perpetuated some five years ago – he subjected them to an attack using obscene chemical weapons. The result? Scores, including children, killed or maimed. The previous time he committed this vile crime, President Barack Obama stated that the Syrian dictator had 'crossed a line', giving the impression that military action – mainly bombing – would take place against the regime in Damascus. Nothing happened. The British response also was craven, though, to his credit, then Prime Minister David Cameron put before Parliament a motion that the RAF should attack Assad's forces. To their discredit, a majority of MPs voted against this justified measure.

Donald Trump, however, rapidly moved from condemnation of this crossing the line, to action – he ordered the bombing of Syrian military installations. The adverse effect on Assad's military prowess was probably minimal, but it could be that at last 'the crocodile' is being put on a diet! It is to be hoped so – fervently.

23

A Failure to Communicate

'WHAT we have here is a failure to communicate';
a famous line from that memorable film, *Cool Hand
Luke*.

The words were voiced by the brutal chief of a prison in
the southern states of the USA and directed at an inmate
whose name features in the title; the charismatic Paul
Newman played the persecuted convict who was to suffer
greatly for this perceived lack of dialogue.

To me such an observation is ever pertinent, certainly as
true and relevant now as it was then and speaks a truth
which causes so much confusion, dislocation, upset,
annoyance – even misery and tragedy. As common an
example of it in everyday life is in the break up of so many
intimate relationships, some lasting for decades. The
majority of us who are in marriages or partnerships talk to
each other – share thoughts, worries, joys – but a
significant number do not and due to this mutual reticence
regarding involving one another, rifts ensue often terminal
to what might have been the closest of unions. It is though,
so avoidable; after all, the bulk of us have the gift of both

speech and hearing – we can articulate problems, concerns, and be informed of those which detract from the happiness of the person with whom we live and whom we love.

Schisms also occur amongst relations, friends and such like because some cannot be bothered – or forget – to involve others in matters which might be of importance to them. Certainly it would appear that too often in, for instance, the workplace, loyal, hard working employees will learn of impending redundancies through reading of it in local newspapers, management having failed to have sufficient thought – indeed, integrity – to warn them of grave possibilities which will, clearly, impact heavily upon the lives of their families and themselves.

Less callous than this, but retrograde nevertheless, is the occasional failure of work colleagues to pass information and advice amongst themselves even though such could be crucial to efficiency, safety and morale. Usually this, like most insularity, is down to lethargy rather than spite or the like, but it can be so detrimental to goodwill and competence. All this, though, whilst both unnecessary and undesirable, does not have, remotely, the seriousness – indeed, potential calamity – of, for instance, the failure of dialogue and disclosures which affect directly people's health and welfare, often their lives.

Hospitals, sadly, are frequently to the fore in this direction; patients of all ages (though the very young and elderly tend to be the most vulnerable) can seemingly become anonymous, invisible even, swallowed by a system where their needs – often urgent – are not catered for. It is probable such situations arise not so often due to indifference of hospital staff (though this can happen) but down, rather, to an insidious lack of communication; the patient's GP not forwarding vital medical history, say, or hospitals not recording such as efficiently as they should; or various departments or wards within these, at times, huge medical 'empires', simply not conversing with each other; if they did it would make their jobs easier and could aid the return of the sick person to health.

However serious situations like these are, there is another scenario one hears of that is even worse. With a frequency which both appals and sickens, we read in the papers, or hear via the media, reports of the most brutal, bestial attacks on children – beatings, torture, starvation even – so often leading to death. Clearly the authorities whose duty it is to detect and prevent such viciousness – police, social workers, doctors and nurses and the like – cannot always be aware of the sufferings of a child within the privacy of the domestic home; yet recurringly it comes out in inquests, enquiries and subsequent trials of the evil men and women who commit these atrocities, that at least one of the official bodies with whom the persecuted child will come into contact will have had suspicions, if not proof, that the boy or girl was the victim of abuse.

The folly, though, is that too often there is a failure on their part to voice concerns to similar agencies employed by the state to – amongst other things – protect the vulnerable. Thus follow avoidable tragedies – then – contrite officials mouthing apologies before ending, almost invariably, with that hackneyed platitude 'Lessons will be learnt'.

Lamentably, rarely do they appear to be; for despite the

sophistication and ubiquity of modem technology, the plight of many continues to 'pass under the radar', largely due to a 'failure to communicate'. It is a culture of incompetence – worse, at times, possibly indifference – which must change; children, especially, deserve so much better.

24

'Nowt So Queer as Folk'

*A*CCORDING to the old northern adage, 'there's nowt so queer as folk'!

It is an observation regarding individual behaviour with which it would be difficult to argue; for the reality is that every member of the human race is unique – even 'identical twins' will not be totally so. They will have, no matter how small, some physical feature different from that of their sibling, some aspect of character, idiosyncrasy, outlook – intelligence even – which will be theirs alone.

Thank heavens for it; whilst science now is moving along a road towards cloning human beings – a disturbing aspect of so called 'progress' – nature is far more democratic, permitting us all to be disparate and contradictory (at times radically so). For instance, I know a fellow who would possibly – if he had the means – have an escalator instead of stairs in his home so careful is he when it comes to expending energy; yet he has run a dozen or so marathons, including the iconic London event, willingly – indeed, enthusiastically – paying a sizeable fee to enter, seemingly enjoying plodding every agonising yard. There is another local chap who is a vegetarian yet contentedly works in an abattoir; and a lady with a glorious voice, a soloist attached to a prominent choir here in the South West, who gives, and gathers much pleasure from using her talent – yet is so nervous before going on stage, she often is physically sick. Mind you, beyond such illogicality and eccentricity, there are on occasions aspects which can be a touch more perverse – indeed anti-social.

For instance, folk campaigning against pollution of the environment whose own gardens and backyards are in a state of neglect – even grime – that would embarrass Albert Steptoe; far more harmfully there are 'animal rights' activists who behave in a mindless, bigoted, criminal way; they 'save' a handful of creatures, but cause the savage deaths of thousands of hapless others. Surely there was never a more vivid act in this direction than when, some years ago, many Mink were 'liberated' into the wild by these terrorists. They multiplied as animals do and proceeded to kill smaller, indigenous, more timid beasts, the vulnerable Water Vole, especially, suffering so greatly they have become an endangered species. Worse still are such people as those who call themselves 'pro-life' yet attack – even murder – medical practitioners who carry out abortions and, most hideously depraved of all, Islamic State and Taliban maniacs who commit the most brutal acts of butchery in the name of religion.

This grotesquely malevolent side to human behaviour should not, however, be permitted to distort the very vital way in which people's foibles, eccentricities, peculiarities, enrich everyday life, strange – at times foolish, even perhaps absurd – opinions, views and actions bringing light relief to the beholder. Recently I overheard a lady, whom I know to be a teacher, grumbling to her companion that she had yet to master the arcane art of learning to drive a car. Her friend suggested she sought the professional tuition of a driving instructor; the reply was a classic – 'oh I've tried them several times; the trouble is they don't leave you alone; they keep telling you what to do!' Clearly an opening here for a coach with no desire to communicate. There is a gent in the area who runs a pub – happily and successfully – despite being a life-long teetotaller, and a fellow I knew back in my younger days who managed to get a position as a lifeguard in a holiday camp, yet could barely swim; fortunately – for him and bathers – his attentions were never required. Do any come more preposterous than the admission from a Church of England Bishop recently, that he felt it ever more difficult to believe in the existence of God? Hopefully his employers find it increasingly problematical paying his salary.

Mind you, ever ready as I am to articulate bizarre behaviour in others it would be hypocritical in the extreme if I were not to gaze into a mirror (hypothetically, that is – I lack the courage to do it literally) and admit to a few daft traits in myself. For instance, as a young man on the family farm, and in these days when ministering to the soil in our garden, I have not the slightest qualms rooting in the rich earth in bare hands; yet always I've had an abhorrence of picking up food with ungloved digits; I shudder at the thought of fingering chips; even a chicken drumstick needs to be attacked with a knife and fork.

Basically I consider myself to be a tolerant man, yet am the possessor of numerous prejudices, plus quirks and illogicalities. To list them all would fill a further column with foolish self-indulgence; readers deserve far better.

25

Shaving

*F*OR many years now I've realised that, although I was ever close to my mother, in terms of character, personality traits, habits and outlook, I am my 'father's son'.

This encompasses numerous aspects of life of varying significance – and as I age I become even more aware of such empathies. One which comes to mind is my lifelong aversion to shaving – a chore which he also found most tiresome. Mind you, there is no way I have ever been able to avoid it as I have an even greater dislike of the consequences, inevitable, of a failure to 'defoliate' one's chin – at first stubble, then, obviously, a beard.

Thus, daily (well most days) the unwanted growth has to be removed; a task which, even though it takes but minutes, to an impatient old toad like me represents precious time wasted – though any lady, of whatever age, reading this will have no sympathy as most of their gender will spend infinitely longer in their preparations to face the day.

As to my father, he viewed the necessity of having to keep a smooth chin with even less sympathy than myself – if that is possible – but being a man of conventional lifestyle, the cut throat razor (a lethal looking weapon, perceptively named) would, most mornings, be criss crossed over his jaw, scraping away the offending black shadow, though being a farmer – thus some days not having to leave the venue where he both dwelt and worked – he might, occasionally, guiltily, forsake the daily ritual. Rarely though, would he venture beyond the farm, even to visit the village for a paper, without employing the miniature scythe upon his reluctant chin. On those occasions when he did, it would be, amongst other matters, to contract out the harvesting of his facial hair to another – the local barber, known to one and all as 'Lou'.

Sometimes, when a young lad, I would ride with him to the village in our old van and end up in Lou's 'salon' watching that genial, patient fellow wield a razor which usually had a cutting edge blunter than a spoon. The word 'salon' is a courtesy title, for it was a cavern-like den with cobwebs stretching back to the reign of Victoria – as indeed, did Lou, and much of the equipment he used. It would not have surprised totally if one espied Charles Dickens wielding his quill pen at a dusty desk, his work illuminated by a guttering candle – such was the 19th century ambience of this archaic barber's shop.

Whilst the great novelist was not in attendance, however, a good number of folk were (all men, naturally), especially in winter when an ancient paraffin heater kept the place warm. Few were there as customers (though they would avail themselves of the proprietor's erratic skills when need dictated) but rather to 'chew the fat' – talk of local events, gossip, politics, sport and such like; this was one of the reasons for my father's attendance, to keep his

*A lifelong aversion to shaving – why does it grow
on the chin where it is unwanted, but not the pate
where it is much desired?*

'finger on the pulse' of life in the parish. Also, despite his clear discomfort of having his chin flayed by a blunt instrument (though still not as brutal as Lou's scissors, memory suggests, when he cut my hair in my youth) it saved Dad from the palaver of doing it himself – and the charge was very low.

My 'old man's' shaving routine remained likewise right up until the time I, at the early age of 14, needed to start myself. I was, though, rescued – almost miraculously – from the worst aspects of the daily torture; it was as if the SAS had arrived. It was not, mind you, military (or divine) intervention that saved my face from a lifetime of dreary scraping – rather the magnificent advancement of science; for there came, during the 1950s, an innovation which to me is amongst those giant forward, and upward, leaps which has advanced mankind throughout the ages. The advent of the wheel, the printing press, the coming of steam power, then of electricity, the splitting of the atom and, in very recent times, the emergence of the silicon chip, are amongst the seismic breakthroughs which have lifted mankind from cave dwelling to space travel; right up alongside these wonders – to me, at least – is the coming of the electric razor.

My father, who had reactionary tendencies when it came to technology (inherited by his youngest son), was uncharacteristically to the fore in purchasing the revolutionary tool; he kindly permitted me to use it. Extravagant fool that I am, I have since bought my own. Regarding hair, though, there is a question the answer to which appears unknown; why does it grow on the chin where it is unwanted, but not the pate where it is much desired?

26

The Driving Licence

*I*N this world there are many possessions and attainments important – often vital – to the pursuing of a fulfilling, happy contented and relatively uncomplicated life.

I would suggest that to a majority of us, the ownership of a driving licence is well to the fore in this category; certainly one appreciates its full worth only when one loses it. This happened to me back in the late 1980s; for some inexplicable reason, I developed a mild neurological problem. It lasted for almost five years – then, literally overnight, disappeared, fortunately never to return. Doctors and specialists were never able to pinpoint what the problem was; thus inevitably were not in a position to prescribe medication which would alleviate matters.

The upshot – demanded by law – was I had my licence revoked and I would not get it back until the authorities were satisfied my scrambled brain had returned to something approaching normality; fair enough – but it certainly caused problems. My job, being peripatetic, was dependent on me 'having wheels' – thus it was lost; I found another, but not easily and with less pay. The upheaval to family and personal life was immense. Here, though, I was blessed in that I am married to the indomitable Ann. Ever doing the manifold range of tasks which came the way of the mother of four sons and the wife of an impractical husband; plus being in full time employment at that time, she had to do the driving also – which was not inconsiderable.

To make matters worse we had teenage twins who were just beginning to learn to drive; heroically she would take them out to practice, at times a terrifying business; that they both passed first time was down, in large measure, to her calmness, perception and nerves of steel (or at least she crucially gave the impression that they were made of such). She has never been fond of being behind the wheel, but she confronted the challenge with stoicism and grit, once in a single day, driving to Sheffield and back – over 600 miles. There are clearly far more draconian disadvantages in life which one can suffer and have to endure than being banned from driving; yet those years are branded deep into my consciousness.

Though not the greatest of drivers at any time – and my proficiency assuredly does not increase with age – I try always to remain within the law. Certainly I attempt, constantly, to be aware that the heaviest part of my anatomy is a leaden right foot, which, if not severely disciplined, can bully an accelerator pedal into a blatant disregard of the statutes on speeding. Our insurance and road tax are always paid on the very same day the reminder arrives; for if such legal requirements are not observed within the short span of time permitted, then a fine will have to be paid. This though, is the lesser of dual penalties; for such misdemeanours mean 'points', which assuredly do not 'win prizes' – the slogan of a television show of yesteryear – but rather, can result in disqualification from driving if 12 or more are accrued within three years.

It is not hard to do – really excessive speeding allied to driving without insurance can achieve it in one go, as can failing a breathalyser test; a minimum of 12 months licence-less follows the latter, and a fortune to be paid for insurance when you're again allowed behind a wheel. Drinking alcohol to a level so low one can drive comfortably within the law is, generally, an art mastered far more effectively by the generations younger than mine. Anybody under the age of 60 would have known nothing other than a world where breathing into a small bag and witnessing part of it turning the wrong colour can bring misery and opprobrium.

Those of my age, however, first drove cars in a very different era, one where, in effect, if you could walk in a reasonably straight line, then you were sober enough to drive a car; no matter how much liquor had been imbibed. Not right, of course – indefensible, in fact, when one looks back; yet this was the way things were; granted there were infinitely fewer vehicles on the roads – especially in the country lanes which were the principal highways along which I steered my old bangers – but I cannot look back upon it all with any sense of pride.

I am fortunate these days that if we are out for a meal or visiting friends, Ann, who drinks little, usually volunteers to drive home – greatly appreciated. Mind you, no matter how assiduously I attempt to stay within the law, there will come a day when 'Father Time' decides the licence should be surrendered. A while away yet – I hope.

97

e

27

Off to the Pictures

I'VE got sixpence, jolly, jolly sixpence, I've got sixpence to last me all my life – I've got tuppence to spend, tuppence to lend, and tuppence to take home to my wife.'

So ran the words of a jingle back in my youth; the pence mentioned were the old kind – 240 to the pound, so even then half a dozen was not a princely sum.

Back when I was a lad, though, it was sufficient to pay for a meal and a night out in Bere Alston. For often in summer, my good parents would give me a 'tanner' and I would happily walk the mile from our farm to the village.

Firstly I'd visit 'Curly' Jack's shop opposite the parish hall, where I would invest a penny on a glass of very fizzy lemonade, before crossing the road to the hall, paid thruppence to the lady at the door (who had the welcoming ambience of a storm trooper) then entered to grab a place on a rock hard bench close to the front. All the seating would face the back wall, which sported a white square upon which the citizens of the peninsula could view the great – or not so brilliant – films coming from Britain and Hollywood each week. The shows were run by a gentleman from Saltash, who clearly had excellent connections. For pictures which would be in London cinemas this week, probably in Plymouth next, would be showing at Bere Parish Hall probably just a fortnight later.

Always the show would commence with adverts, which would be followed by a couple of shorts – perhaps a cartoon, or the Three Stooges, the Bowery Boys or famed comedy duos such as Abbott and Costello. On a good night it would be my favourites, the hapless Laurel and Hardy. Then the main feature; the widest of gamuts – gangster tales, the Ealing comedies, war films both British and American made (the former vastly more popular as the 'Yanks' and John Wayne winning the war tended to irritate young and old alike), dramas and, of course, westerns.

Strangely I was never a huge fan of them as a genre, but two remain in my memory. *Shane*, starring Alan Ladd, and the picture which, until recently, was in my view the best I ever saw, *High Noon*. It won the Oscar for best actor for the charismatic Gary Cooper; there was also an accolade for the theme ballad, the mesmeric *Do Not Forsake Me Oh My Darling*. Even though just a lad, the message from this brilliant film was not lost on me that it is not only nations which appease, but individuals and communities likewise. The evil 'Frank Miller' is returning on the noon train to once again (along with his cohorts), terrorise the people of 'Hadleyville'. Yet nobody is willing to help the marshal (Cooper) repel them. Such a long lasting effect did the production have on me, I purchased, years back, the video, then the DVD and still watch it.

After the show, the final two pennies of my funds were spent on chips from the 'chippie' some 50 yards from the hall. Then, replete both physically and mentally, I would trundle home. For many years after this I was a regular cinema goer, mainly to Tavistock and Plymouth, the rather basic facilities of the parish hall unable to compete with the coming of television.

In recent times I've been a relatively rare picture attender as the cosy armchair at home tends to have greater allure than the cinema. However, a few weeks ago I was persuaded to join the family in a visit to a 'multi-screen' in Plymouth (the word 'multi' being very apt, as the auditoriums stretched as far as the eye could see). I'm glad I went, for I witnessed a picture, which, to me, was even finer than *High Noon*.

It was noisy, violent, brutal, tragic, terrifying – yet at the same time, awesome, magnificent, mind-concentrating, breathtaking, heroic – a memorable tribute to the valiance of so many in our great nation.

If *Dunkirk* does not win the Oscar, BAFTA, indeed every award there is for best picture then, assuredly, there is little justice.

28

Musing on Christmas-time

*I*T is almost here, the Yuletide; some folk dislike it intensely while possibly a similar percentage love it dearly and spend months (and much money) preparing for it.

When it comes, their sole regret is that it passes far too quickly.

The majority, however, probably lie somewhere in between.

We grumble about the cost of it, the hassle (perhaps, at times, the anxiety which it can induce), but when it arrives generally we enjoy it – the singing of carols, the parties, families getting together (though such can be a mixed blessing), good food, generous amounts of liquor and, of course, the presents.

For children, clearly, it is a magical time. A few weeks before the event, the temperature of expectation and excitement rockets.

There are nativity plays (some, it has to be said, with little reference to the birth of Christ), parties, pantomimes, the raising of a Christmas tree and its decorations, the incessant tsunami of advertisements spewing from televisions exhorting the buying of gifts ranging from the exotic to the tawdry, the serious to the daft, the bargain to the exorbitant. Then, at last for youngsters, the most enchanting night of the year – Christmas Eve and the coming of Father Christmas.

As a small boy my faith in the existence of this red garbed, white bearded gentleman was total, largely because it was never betrayed.

For the following morning would find the ample stocking at the foot of my bed filled with a fine array of gifts, all of which were a delight.

Mind you, the pile of 'goodies' then would have been a mole hill compared to the mountain which will dwarf the beds of most youngsters in these generally more affluent and material times. Back then, to be fair, Santa's resources were far more limited; large numbers of his 'helpers' and 'elves' would have been conscripted into the war effort, possibly building spitfires, working down the mines, 'Digging for Victory' or donning uniform to fight for King and Country.

In consequence, supplies of toys and the like which would bring joy to children were severely limited.

The sole aspect of positivity in this was that democracy (in theory, at least), held sway as shortages and deprivation were endured by rich and poor alike, though in reality, the latter were a touch more likely to suffer them.

All this is a very long time ago, as is my belief in the existence of this portly, jovial, brightly hued character – and his reindeer – who is based, reportedly, in Lapland.

Yet, cynical though I am regarding the reality of this fine fellow, I'll not tempt fickle fate too much by categorically denying his existence.

For every Christmas morning on my side of the bed, there will be a vital addition to my beleaguered drinks cabinet, usually bearing the glorious words, 'single malt'.

Also perhaps, a box of quality chocolates to massage and comfort a palate which ever craves sugar; calorie laden bliss.

Now our chimney is far too narrow to allow the entry of a largish fellow, while the roof tiles would surely show signs of damage if a heavy sleigh pulled by hefty reindeer was parked upon it.

Mind you there would also be droppings, which could be useful for the garden!

So from where do these so welcome gifts come? I suspect they could be delivered by female hands.

Perhaps – Mother Christmas? Why not? She would probably be slimmer than the traditional male, thus able to get down the chimney and possibly be of a more practical environmentally friendly outlook, thus drop down on roofs in a small hot air balloon or the like.

It is also said that women are far better at organising and multitasking than the male of the species (no comment).

Assuredly, with multitudes of gifts to make in a brief time, followed by worldwide distribution in a single night (well beyond 'Amazon' even with the use of drones), such qualities are crucial.

Whatever, as nobody is able ever to see this famed figure, gender will remain a mystery; Not important – just as long as somebody drops in.

A happy, stress-free Yuletide to one and all.

29

Democracy

*T*HE dictionary describes democracy as a 'form of government in which sovereign power resides in the people as a whole.' Could anything be fairer – or clearer? – one would think not. Yet it is with sadness – and unease – that I opine, respectfully, we do not in these times treasure, sufficiently, this precious, egalitarian procedure. Much is made of the threat to our freedoms posed by, say, Putin's Russia, Islamic extremism and terrorism in general. I would suggest, however, that whilst peril can come to Britain from such directions, possibly more threaten from within.

Although now an old man who has been favoured in having lived a fulfilling life, it does not mean I gaze back at the past through distorted lenses of a 'rose tinted' hue; yet the conviction has been growing within me for probably a decade and more now, that the understanding of, and tolerance for our precious democracy is increasingly under threat. Not that modern Britain is awash with anarchists whose ambitions are to destroy the settled, staple, elected means of government which has evolved over the centuries; No, it is from honest citizens themselves – a fair percentage, anyway – that the danger emanates.

Such folk are not troublemakers or revolutionaries; rather they are decent men and women, hard working, caring, responsible, essentially law abiding. The problem, though, is that a growing number seem unable (at times, perhaps, unwilling) to come to terms with the core values and responsibilities of the democratic process. Elected representatives of the people, from 'grass roots' to Westminster, have within their ranks an escalating quota who fail to comprehend the altruistic, principled nature of this process (as defined above).

For instance, someone is elected or co-opted onto a local council; perhaps they have suggestions, ideas, projects which they feel, if adopted, will benefit the community; at times they will oppose existing policies which, in their view, are detrimental and which should be confronted by councillors. Their notions become motions and, following debate, are put to fellow members; a vote is held. Their proposals lack majority support; do they then shrug their shoulders and move on? Most do, but too many in these times simply resign their seat, often claiming their positive ideas are ignored by a reactionary cabal. This cavalier, almost subversive action, means public money has to be spent on electing a replacement, plus, even more crucially, for a period local residents will have fewer councillors representing them.

It does not end at parish and district level, mind you, for many MPs would seem to have scant respect for the will of the people. Could anything exemplify this more than the reaction of a sizeable minority of those elected to parliament, regarding the outcome of the referendum of June 2016. The nation was given power, directly, to decide if they wished the United Kingdom to remain part of the European Union. By a clear majority the people instructed both government and parliament to lead our country out of this organisation, 'leave' voters ascendent in over 70% of the electoral districts throughout the United Kingdom. Most MPs, no matter what their personal views, bowed to the popular will, proceeding to bring forward the legislation which would put the nation onto the path of independent sovereignty once more.

A significant rump though, appear imbued with the patronising arrogance that they, sitting in the Palace of Westminster, know what is best for citizens and country alike. This attitude and mindset, that those dwelling in our land cannot be trusted to make decisions which affect its future, either nationally or locally (unless, of course, it accords with their own views) is dangerous, divisive, even seditious. It is an imperiousness and condescension which offends – and undermines our basic rights.

The nation which gave the world the concept of common law plus the foundations of freedom under it – enshrined in Magna Carta – and which has sacrificed so much in defence of liberty, deserves better from those privileged to speak for it.

30

Gatwick to JFK

*I*T was an early start – we had to be at Gatwick by 2pm. At 8.30am a car pulled up outside our house; a gentleman alighted and greeted us. Rapidly our cases were stored in the boot and we were off, Ann in the back seat where she was able to do a cryptic crossword (beyond my capabilities), myself in the front.

I was privileged to be sitting beside a most affable fellow; soon we were discussing the state of the nation, general idiosyncracies of life – and Plymouth Argyle, he, like myself, being a devoted follower.

For very many years, of course, such debate would lead to a despairing shake of the head, even a 'wailing and gnashing' of teeth. Not this time, though, for a few days earlier they had achieved promotion for the first time in 13 years; joy abounded.

Stopping only for a 'comfort break', we moved quite seamlessly towards our destination. However, as we motored up the M3 – including the multi-mile stretch cursed with roadworks and speed restrictions which seem to have existed since they first started building Stonehenge – a silence engulfed us. For we were approaching an area where, on an ancient map, could well have been written – 'Here be dragons'; in these times the terrain is terrorised by a tarmaced monster – the M25 motorway. Would it be benign or roaring with the combined ferocity of a multitude of exhausts? Might it be, as so often is the case, the nation's longest car park?

Hallelujah – traffic was moving freely; Gatwick loomed – and was soon reached.

So far, so good in our journey to New York to visit our son Matthew, daughter-in-law Avisa, and trio of grandchildren. From there on though, matters were less positive. Due to restrictions we could not be dropped in the designated area. Thus we staggered some considerable distance across roads and car parks heaving heavy cases; at last, we espied the terminal and found a lift which would take us up to it. Eventually it did but only at the third time of asking, twice taking us to the wrong levels. The baggage check was without hitch – but that regarding security was not. As instructed I placed wallet, car keys, coins and top coat into a tray which trundled on rollers into a tunnel to be scanned; it failed to reappear! Panic – what was happening; did I look like a terrorist? Were these crucial requirements being confiscated? Thankfully no. There had been a 'traffic jam' in the tunnel; great relief. Coffee having been imbibed, we were invited to our flight gate and were soon aboard the aircraft; USA – here we come! Well, not quite.

We were belted up; aircraft engines were throbbing – yet no take off. Twenty minutes passed – no movement. At last, a message from the captain; apologies – all was ready for the 'off' but they were awaiting a form which he had to sign before they could go.

_No tea or coffee! – If there had been a
parachute nearby, I'd have used it._

'Just a few minutes more,' said he. A quarter of an hour later, a further epistle; 'Sorry, ladies and gentlemen, for the delay – we have received the form but it was the wrong one.' My inherent impatience was coming to the fore – and I was not alone. Before it reached boiling point, the plane began to move; clearly the form saga was at an end. We were never told what this official document concerned; perhaps it was an MOT certificate – or, on the other hand, one to say that the aircraft had failed. It's doubtful anybody cared – the wheels were turning; there was a problem though, in that they continued to turn; onwards, sideways – possibly even backwards – the mighty machine moved, its destination a runway from which to take off.

So long did it take, one can only assume the point of departure was situated somewhere near Truro. At last, though, we were airborne – some 70 minutes late. The flight itself was largely uneventful; however, the food was disappointing. One does not expect Cordon Bleu catering on an aircraft – but here it was really substandard; and there was a calamity. For in mid-Atlantic we were informed that due to a technical problem, there would be no tea or coffee. If there had been a parachute nearby, I'd have used it.

Eventually, JFK airport; almost there – but not quite. It seems harder to get into the United States than it is to escape from prison. An endless wait in passport control, then fingerprints taken, plus a grilling from a charmless official. This hurdle scaled, there was a half hour wait to retrieve baggage. Such gathered at last by weary, though relieved hands; we staggered out to be welcomed by our dear Avisa – 90 minutes later. The holiday had begun.

31

New York – New York

'NEW York, New York – It's so good they named it twice;' So the song goes. Now just how fine it is has to be a matter of opinion, but like all great world cities it has a flavour and culture of its own. The largest conglomerate in the United States, located in a state of like name, is big, confident and densely populated.

Ann and I visited there some years ago when son Matthew was last in the 'new world'. Then he was living in Manhattan, the pulsating heart of a multi-race city which according to the above mentioned song 'never sleeps'. We enjoyed our stay then but were pleased that Matt, along with daughter-in-law Avisa plus their delightful children (Elahe, Salma and Kasra) having returned to work in the 'big apple' have settled in the suburbs, a more tranquil environment. At our age relative peace and quiet has an appeal that pulsating life cannot match.

The hospitality and consideration of our hosts was, as always, magnificent. A most comfortable home (and bed), imaginative delicious food and a supply of wines and beverages that, most agreeably, outstripped demand. Their kindness and forethought ensuring that we were equipped with bus, train and subway tickets to travel around the city, along with detailed guidance how to get to places, proved to be as crucial as it was appreciated.

Ann is much better at following signs and directions than I, a man who could get lost in a phone box, but neither of us would have braved the city on our own without such shrewd counsel. Various forays were made, but none more fraught, though necessary, than a trip to 'Ground Zero' deep in the bowels of the metropolis. Our destination was reached thanks to a series of travelling triumphs which are a matter of some pride. We caught the correct bus to the station, then ascertained the right platform (granted there were but two) and got aboard the relevant conveyance which in theory would take us to the heart of this mighty town; it did. Grand Central Station is a travel hub seemingly the size of a small county; from here a subway train would deliver us to Broadway (theatre land).

A few hundred yards away from there is the evocative memorial and museums dedicated to the horrors, and, by many, valiant rescue efforts, involved in that monstrous act of vindictive evil which took the lives of so many 16 years ago. To say the memorials are moving is an understatement; one certainty – this unforgivable apocalyptic atrocity will not be forgotten, nor will its victims. In the profound words of Virgil printed boldly on a wall – 'No day shall erase you from the memory of time'.

Other visits were made, firstly to the home of President Franklin Roosevelt some miles from the city. Here was his family home plus large impeccably appointed buildings in which, using both film and this great man's written and recorded words, his crucial contribution to twentieth century history is displayed. Not far from here stands a mansion once in the ownership of the, at one time, fabulously wealthy Vanderbilt family. Amongst many recollections of this visit is a modern sign instructing visitors – 'do not bring fire arms into the house'; not often seen outside National Trust houses one suspects!

One afternoon we went to watch baseball, New York Yankees versus Baltimore Orioles. This was an experience, an episode of American life, tastes and culture which demands and will be receiving an article all to itself at a later date. Sufficient to say that in my view – granted, far from an expert one – few things exemplify the diversity in attitude and approach to life in our countries than the differing priorities and passions involved in professional sport in Britain and the USA.

There are other areas where it is clear old world and new are so very divergent. George Bernard Shaw suggested Britain and the United States are 'nations separated by a common language'. It's no good asking the location of the nearest petrol station – gas is their word, of course. The gents or ladies is the 'rest room', drivers do not give way at a junction, rather they adopt passivity, so 'yield'. Crisps are 'crackers', biscuits are 'cookies', trousers are 'pants', nappies, 'diapers' and dustbins 'trash cans'. The list is endless. Annoying to my English eyes is their spelling, absolutely atrocious.

Then there are pavements called 'sidewalks'; the mystery, however, is why any are laid, for so few people seem to use them. The automobile dominates here more, probably, than in any other country on earth and they still drive on the wrong side of the road!

But that's their business; the actuality is we had a fulfilling visit to five much treasured members of our beloved family – and we will return.

32

Baseball

'*L*ET'S all go to the ball game' – Such are the words in a famous old American song.

This is what we did, Ann and I, one Sunday lunchtime; not, however, to our usual destination for such a pursuit – the hallowed stands and turf of Home Park, Plymouth. No – this was to a vast stadium in a metropolis on another continent; and it was not to see the sport graced by the likes of Matthews, Pelé and Messi, but that which brought fame and fortune to such as Joe DiMaggio and Mickey Mantel.

The Yankee Stadium, situated in the heart of The Bronx, a rather rundown part of New York City, was the venue, and the ball at the heart of matters was no bigger than that used for cricket; New York Yankees were home to Baltimore Orioles in major league baseball. Our son Matthew felt that the lives of Ann and I in the 'Big Apple', where he and our daughter-in-law Avisa are working, would be enhanced if we, for an afternoon, immersed ourselves in traditional American sporting culture. It was assuredly 'an experience'.

The home of this famous baseball club is vast – almost Wembley-like in scale. Yet unlike the iconic London arena, which has numerous entry points, this appeared to have but one. That was not hard to locate, for the queue shuffling towards it stretched, seemingly, miles. We joined it – seven in all, including the grandchildren. Well before we gained entry it was clear, from the noise, the game had started.

Eventually we reached the entrance to be confronted by security gates and scanners; if ever the phrase 'going through the motions' was accurate this was such a time. Some people were subjected to a quite rigorous search of possessions and person, others to little more than a cursory glance. Fortunately I was among the latter; possibly the uniformed official thought I looked too old and senile to pose a threat to anyone.

Having at last accessed the stadium, there followed a trudge, onwards and upwards, to our seats, hundreds of steps away. At last arriving there almost exhausted, I had a desire to plant a Union Jack and claim it for Queen and Country; this though, in a land which flies its flag like no other, would have not gone down well.

We started to watch the game – it was not easy; partly this was because the rules are, to me, a total mystery, but also the fact the crowd appeared constantly to be on the move. Folk were leaving their seats to buy vital supplies to sustain them for the duration of the match – upwards of four hours; others having purchased, were shuffling back carrying buckets (literally in terms of size) of popcorn, French fries, chicken nuggets, burgers, doughnuts, hot dogs, cola, beer, ice cream and much more.

The concourses at the back of the stands were awash with jostling humanity, queueing to buy victuals of sufficient quantity to possibly keep a decent sized army going for months; the atmosphere was that of Goose Fair.

The major sporting event taking place on the 'Diamond' down below us seemed to be semi-ignored, spectators giving the occasional cheer between the swallowing of mouthfuls of food. Not Matt, however; like any true Briton he 'takes his pleasures seriously' which includes sport. A fellow of immense patience, he attempted to instill in Ann and myself the rudiments of this arena game which seemed sparse in riveting action. With his mother he made excellent progress, with me, none. Not witnessing sight or sign of goalposts, wickets, cues or racquet, I was lost. Matt, aided by Ann, spent much of the long afternoon trying to enlighten me but to no avail. I was as ignorant at the end as at the beginning. The only knowledge I departed with was the scoreline – the home team, second in the league table, had been defeated by the visitors, lying third. Not that many Yankees' fans seemed particularly fussed or downcast over the result; mind you such were not numerous at the end, an initial 'gate' of over 41,000 reducing to probably a third at the time play concluded.

It seemed as if some folk paid their entrance fee (not small), bought their feast, devoured it, gave a couple of token cheers to support their team then went home – probably for tea. We did likewise at the end; speaking personally, I left a touch disappointed. It had been interesting but lacked noticeably the fervour of British sport. Having been marinated in the 'tribal' passions and loyalties of English league football, the occasion was devoid of drama and theatre; the result, even to real supporters, did not seem to be of major importance. To sports devotees this side of 'the pond' winning is vastly more crucial than eating.

117

33

Birthdays

A GENT I know, of similar vintage to myself, recently experienced a birthday.

Now usually the word 'celebrated' would be employed to mark this annual event in our lives, but in this instance it would be inappropriate as it is assuredly inaccurate. For all he did was grumble about it, seeing it as another year older, a further significant step along the path leading, inevitably, towards the scythe of the Grim Reaper.

In reality, this is correct; however, no matter what one's age, the fact is every anniversary of the day one entered the world, inexorably moves us in the direction of the moment we are destined to leave it, so why worry about it? Now my own birthday is not well timed – just before Christmas.

There are occasions – though rare, it must be said – when I feel a touch guilty about this; after all, immediately pre-Yuletide there are manifold demands on the hours and purses of the family, thus such a personal anniversary must be at least an unwelcome distraction, perhaps even a nuisance.

Rapidly, though, I do rationalise that whilst I'm to blame for many follies in my life, this is not one of them; the date of my entering this mortal coil had nothing to do with me. Thus I enjoy the day each year when my maturity advances officially; I always have to a large extent, but strangely, as I get ever older, I tend to relish it more. Possibly it is the fact that the marking of another 12 months represents something of a triumph – though I have yet to reach a longevity concerning which I will afflict folk by boasting of it. Invariably I have a good day – Ann and the family see to that.

She will always bake a cake or sponge of sheer delight, and stick a few candles on the top – a token gesture this, for if it were to sport an accurate number, the surface would need to be the size of a helicopter pad, and the heat generated would finish off the already threatened polar ice caps.

If young grandchildren are about, the flames will be extinguished by a hurricane of breath more charged with moisture than the average sprinkler system; such, though, will in no way deter this serial dessert consumer from devouring a slice (let's be honest – slices) of enormous size and weight.

Then there are the presents; my sons and daughters-in-law and, of course, my wonderful wife, know my tastes so well – with 'taste' being the relevant word.

My bundle of gifts will, generally, be sockless, tieless, shirtless indeed usually, slipperless, though being the possessor of feet which can be colder than marble even in June, they certainly would not be unwelcome.

Valiant attempts to warm such extremities are made in

the shape of bottles – whisky, brandy, port; I'm not sure the imbibing of such actually get down to the toes, but it certainly warms everything else – and it evokes in me a relaxation, positivity and a spirit of goodwill towards all folk (well, most anyway); and if the 'pressie' cannot be drunk then usually it will be edible, my self-destructive teeth-rotting passion for chocolate being indulged most generously.

There is a further pleasure to the day even greater than the 'goodies' – welcome and valued calls from our four sons. One lives locally so will almost certainly drop in, whilst the other three – two dwelling in the south east at present, the third in New York – will telephone.

Overall there will be warm, congenial talk on many topics, though early on a most depressing subject will be got out of the way – Plymouth Argyle.

Selfishly I brainwashed my lads at an early age to follow the Pilgrims, so no conversation between us can take place without some mention of the current disasters tormenting Home Park. Despite this, my spirits are always boosted after talking with them – as they are, over all, following this day I enjoy immensely.

So, I'm hoping for a few more yet plus the liquor, of course – and visits and calls from my so very loyal family.

34

The Twin Savage Serpents

*B*EING a somewhat obtuse chap, there have always been numerous aspects of human behaviour, habits, outlook and beliefs, which have puzzled – at times baffled me. As age does not sharpen either senses or brain power, such bemusement engulfs me with increasing regularity. At present none perplex me more than two issues which are pertinent over the airwaves, media and in parliament. Although our awareness of such increase daily, there remains, seemingly, bewilderment as to what to do to rectify matters. I refer to the twin savage serpents which now, and historically, have all too often perverted justice and fairness in our national life – racism and sexism.

Both attitudes have perpetually mystified. Why somebody should suffer discrimination and prejudice because of the colour of their skin, their religion or creed; has ever escaped me. It is baffling – perhaps, tragic – that despite the fact people travel now as they never have before, see other countries, rub shoulders with a wide range of humanity, have means of communication of the

f

highest sophistication, this destructive antagonism to some of one's fellow citizens still exists – indeed, in places, flourishes. Mind you, I am a nationalist; I have always been proud and privileged to be British and would never wish to be anything other. However, although I am caucasian, my 'white' skin does not make me any more legitimate as a native of these islands than those whose colour is of a different hue, or adhere to a non-Christian religion. As long as they swear allegiance to Queen and country, are guided by our laws, then to me, they are all part of the mighty family of Britons.

The other spike in this two pronged attack on equality and fair play in our realm, and beyond, is gender inequality. Here we are, well into the 21st century, yet in very many ways the female of the species still are treated as second class citizens – even in our own fair state, the mother of all democracies, the creator of the noble concept of common law.

In a comprehensive range of activities women are denied equity with men. Not officially, of course; in law, they have rights to the same pay, opportunities and freedom of expression. Yet all around, in manifold directions, women are confronted with obstacles and barriers which are rarely thrust into the paths of males. Some religions (not totally excluding Christianity) obstruct female equality in ideological dictates, but across the full panorama of life ingrained discrimination still corrupts justness.

Most groups, employers, organisations, and the like, mouth full support for equal chances and rewards for the distaff side but so many fail to deliver. Even those whose purpose was, and is, to fight for workers' interests, such as trade unions, have not always fulfilled their role, they, at times, having negotiated pay rates higher for men than for women.

Looking back, I realise that so much of my antagonism – anger, even – regarding the present day lack of even-handedness between the sexes, goes back to my youth. For the local world in which I was brought up was based solidly upon equality, no matter what the gender. My parents were farmers – the way of life of my family for many generations. However, to refer to my mother as a 'Farmer's Wife' would have been an inaccurate description, for it would tend to cast her in a supporting role rather than the principal one she actually held. For she was a farmer. In most aspects of animal husbandry, rural skills, overall knowledge (including horticulture which was a prominent part of their living) she was a match for my father, at the very least. Mind you, my marriage is somewhat different to my father's. For during the almost 50 years I have had the good fortune of being wedded to Ann, I am aware that our happy union has lacked equality: in temperament, abilities, skills, reliability, common sense and intelligence, she has perpetually surpassed myself. A devoted, loving, steadfast Wife and Mother, she is the rock upon which my sons and myself have built our lives; and before she retired from her employment, she was always a higher earner than myself – which helped finances immensely. In all this, I doubt our marriage is unique.

So let us look at truths: We dwell in a great country where the Prime Minister is a woman, and likewise the First Minister for Scotland. Our Head of State – possibly the most famous and respected person in the world – is also a Wife and Mother. No more discrimination – please.

35

Scaffold-stock

*I*T has been suggested by some folk of a cynical mindset that the famous old port and harbour, Padstow, should be renamed 'Stein-stow' – after internationally famed chef and businessman Rick Stein.

Certainly this high profile resident has brought vast amounts of publicity, business and tourists to this old North Cornwall resort and has, in consequence, boosted the income of the area.

As is ever the case, some will have benefited, others not – there are those who are pleased, but many resent that the nature and traditional charm of this old coastal settlement has been changed radically – and arguably for the worse.

Here in Tavistock, we have experienced recently, and during a very brief period of time, a phenomenon pleasing to very few, but one which could also create a movement towards renaming. For hundreds of years the dominant feature of this ancient stannary town – the River Tavy – has been reflected in its title; in recent weeks, though, the famously fast flowing waterway has been overshadowed –

often literally and somewhat alarmingly – by a modern, metallic, meandering menace which has led to putative suggestions that a change of name would be descriptively appropriate – the birthplace of Sir Francis Drake should be called 'Scaffold-stock'.

The logic of such a title is there for all to see, for the town appears to be shrouded in a web-like proliferation of steel stays and supports, some reaching seemingly to the skies. They hold up acres of wooden walkways with planks so numerous that if put end to end they would possibly reach New Zealand.

Certainly in this environmentally conscious age there will be those majority unimpressed by the decimation of forests – which has to be the upshot of providing this plethora of timber.

Mind you, the nation's ailing steel industry will have had a welcome boost with the demand there will have been to provide the multitudinous lengths of piping rising from the pavements in support of the intimidating, uncompromising lace style 'limpets' clinging to walls, ancient and modern; and this is a relevant aspect of the 'triffid' like invasion, the fact that the age of a building – or the fact it is a shop, business or private dwelling – seems to have no relevance when it comes to its enmeshment.

Public piles, some council owned, largish multiple stores, locally owned outlets, apartments all would appear to be tyrannised by the scaffold leviathan.

There are, of course, questions to be asked regarding the quite sudden manifestation. Firstly, who has erected it all?

There's something of a mystery here, for whilst the occasional gent (and it would appear to be a male preserve) has been seen shouldering bits and pieces, so much of the entanglement appears, seemingly, overnight. Perhaps some folk 'work at it' during the hours of darkness, but if they do, it's strange nobody hears them; it could be that some malevolent spirits or trolls, with a grudge, raise it all – or, even, perhaps this domineering trellis has its own means of procreation.

However, if it is a mystery as to how it all got there, the reason for its assembly is possibly an even greater one. Many of the structures to which it clings seem to be in a reasonable state of repair, though I must concede that a man of such lamentable ignorance in practical matters as myself has no right to be listened to in this area; what is more relevant, though, is the fact that little action can be seen upon these temporary (one assumes) ramparts.

If the buildings are in dire need of love and attention, then the elevated planks should be alive with craftsmen, all busying themselves restoring properties once more to good health. Yet one is more likely to see pigeons than people walking the planks. The occasional person has been seen, but generally they have been carrying a clipboard rather than a trowel.

Still, 'what cannot be cured has to be endured'; the 'Dunkirk spirit' is already coming to the fore, with some resilient folk in a town rarely afflicted with drought, viewing matters positively. For instance, it is now possible to walk along pavements generally protected from the rain, the long stretches of roofing provided by planks being, except for the odd drip, a reasonable shield.

Also, it brings a touch of excitement to otherwise routine shopping in that with windows and signs cloaked

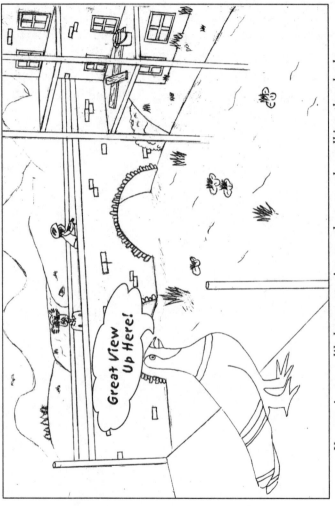

Yet one is more likely to see pigeons than people walking the planks.

in tarpaulin and the like, entering an outlet is something of an adventure as one is never certain what is for sale until entry has been made.

However, overall this enforced anonymity can be no aid to trade – or to much else, in reality. Mind you, if the town remains besieged by the synthetic version of Japanese knotweed come December, there could be a small bonus – Dickensian Evening will largely be staged undercover.

36

Putin & the Weather

VLADIMIR Putin, who did not totally astonish the watching world by being re-elected President of Russia, is clearly no friend of the west, especially the United Kingdom.

He means us harm and will resort to a wide and possibly innovative range of tactics to inflict it; these will – and do – include cyber attacks, the vile use of poisons, chemical weapons, harassment of ex-patriots, false news, mis-information, propaganda, threats and other devious, malicious actions aimed at wounding us in these islands.

It would seem, though, rather unlikely that he will offer a direct armed threat; he will posture, mind you (indeed, he already does), but the reality is that militarily, though dangerous, present day Russia is infinitely weaker than the old Soviet Union.

The fact this vast country is relatively feeble economically means their bellicose leader lacks the means, financially, to build his forces to the level which probably he desires. A further relevant factor is one of numbers. The land ruled by Putin has a population little more than half of what it was when the old Soviet empire glowered at the west. Yet is would surely be unwise to believe that this bullying man, with this Stalinist mentality, could, or would, never attempt to launch reasonably conventional armed attacks on our islands. However, being a shrewd fellow, he might not rush into it; probably he would be aware that no aggressive nation has successfully invaded our great country for almost a thousand years.

Many have tried, of course – the Spanish with their mighty armada, the Dutch, the French under the leadership of Napoleon and, in more recent times, that most militaristic of races (back then, at least), Hitler's Nazi Germany. Due to the valiance and resilience of the British people, all have been repelled, though usually due only to great sacrifices from our citizenry in all directions – including the loss of numerous lives.

Now, if the Russian 'Emperor' is as cunning and clever as he appears to be, he will study history, something few folk seem to do – which can be foolish, for it is said those who fail to learn the mistakes of the past are destined to repeat them.

So, if Vladimir thinks along these lines he will research, minutely, the landmark attempts to subjugate we British which have punctuated the centuries. If he does, he might well spend as much effort planning the timing of these large scale sorties, as he does the actual size and tactics of his invading forces; and in this direction, his meteorological office will possibly be as vital as his military advisors.

Mind you, although ruthless, it's doubtful he'll be as brutal to a weatherman as was the terrifying Joseph Stalin back in the 1940s, who had one poor chap shot because it literally 'rained on his parade' when the 'expert's' initial prediction was that it would bask in sunshine.

Russia's president will expect accurate information concerning the climate situation though – but in Britain, rather than his own massive land and it is our winter months which might be of most interest to him.

For if he has analysed, season wise, when aggressors unsuccessfully threatened these 'sceptred' isles, he will realise it was generally done during summer months.

Such was the case the last time our nation confronted an alarming enemy – one which many feared would subjugate us – almost 80 years ago; the Luftwaffe sent hordes of bombers and fighters to hammer us into submission. Thanks to the heroism of the British people in general, and the RAF in particular, the Nazis were repulsed magnificently.

Possibly relevant, though, to the scheming, malevolent mind of Putin, is that the Battle of Britain was fought July to September.

When we turned the tide in 1944, our invasion of Europe came in June. Now, true all this was long ago, yet it is possibly fair to ask, even with modern technology, how well we would handle an attack in winter.

The chaos which ensued following the snow we've experienced recently prompts such a question. Could our fighter planes take off from snow bound airfields? Could our army mobilise – and people cope despite the hazards of ice ridden, vehicle strewn roads, non-functioning railways, electricity lines down, food supplies running low?

The answer is 'yes'. We are an indomitable race that has overcome far more. It would help, though, that if Putin ever does send his aggressors, they come after Easter and before the clocks go back!

37

The Things One Hears

THROUGHOUT virtually all of my life – certainly since
my early teens – I have been fascinated by words,
phrases and sayings.

Some have been from the lips (or pens) of eminent men
and women, but many from people one meets in everyday
life. The range of such expressions is immense; the cynical,
wise, witty, profound, perceptive, gentle, perhaps, at times,
cruel – all those and more have come to my notice, and
whilst I've forgotten many, numerous remain with me.

The inspiring rhetoric of Sir Winston Churchill, with his
defiant promise that 'We will fight them on the beaches,'
and so forth; the electrifying, rhythmic tones of Martin
Luther King and his energising of the Afro-American
people with his unforgettable, 'I have a dream' speech,
those four words repeated numerous times with a power
and passion which gave hope to millions; such come to
mind instantly, as do several others from statesmen,
religious figures and the like.

Yet over the years I have regularly heard copious quips,
comments, asides, observations – often voiced with

simplicity, brevity but deep insight – which have varied from the whimsical to the incisive, the hilarious to the damning.

Well to the fore in the final grouping was a comment made by a councillor some years ago – one completely without guile – regarding a sculpture, commissioned by the authority, to stand in a prime position outside what was then a new and, subsequently, much valued theatre-come-arts centre and cinema in Tavistock.

This creation, the work of a lauded local artist, was most certainly of the 'modern' school and not to everyone's taste, or understanding. Shamefully not long after it was put in place, some anti-social misfit vandalised it.

This wretched news, given to a meeting of the full council, was greeted with bemused shakings of the head, and widespread condemnation. One elderly councillor, however, rose with a puzzled expression on his face, and posed a simple, innocent question; 'But, Mr Mayor – how could they tell?'!

So many quips and observations are pertinent to public and civic life – a majority usually of a somewhat cynical nature.

One which comes to mind is the all too true adage, spoken to me long ago, that 'it is better to shut up and be thought a fool, than to speak up and prove it'. Sadly I have not always adhered to it.

Some maxims are of a positive nature, such as 'where there's a will, there's a way', but probably a majority take a more weary view of life.

A gent I knew some years ago would opine, when reality shattered his ambitions for a relaxed, gentle existence, 'I thought, when young, that life was beauty, but then I found that life was duty.'

My habitually bleak view of the world tends to lead me towards remembering the jaundiced and downbeat sayings and phrases of our language rather than those of a positive nature, despite there being many, of course.

Films, to me, have produced memorable ones; two which come to mind register a highly sceptical approach to relationships between the genders – especially the, at times, somewhat irrational behaviour of a man when wooing a woman.

In that fine film, *My Fair Lady*, the misogynistic Professor Higgins points out, in song, the calamities which can befall a previously happy man when 'You let a woman in your life'.

In another Hollywood musical, *Guys and Dolls*, it is claimed in a memorable number that if a fellow is behaving in eccentric fashion, perhaps even irrationally, 'That the guy's only doing it for some doll.'

To me, though, the most memorable cynical lines in a picture were spoken in that enjoyable western, *The Magnificent Seven*; when remonstrated with by the leader of the 'goodies' (Yul Brynner), who had brought his 'seven' to protect hapless Mexican peasants from constant predatory raids by bandits, their chief – wonderfully played by the late Eli Wallach – states sardonically, 'If God had not meant them to be shorn, he'd not have made them sheep'.

A despicable outlook, of course, but a brilliant bit of writing as in just 15 words it exposes the cold-blooded amorality of somebody happy to exploit others. Sadly there are many such in the world today; fortunately though, there are still more who give rather than take.

38

Self-indulgence

RECENTLY I listened to a sermon condemning the sin of self-indulgence in material matters.

The Preacher was eloquent but there was much she said with which I disagreed. For the gratification condemned could be classed merely as a touch of personal pampering; it did not harm others.

Why should a rich man not buy a Rolls Royce or a wealthy woman adorn herself in the best of fashion?

Surely no reason, as long as they pay their taxes, respect others and look after their families.

There's no way Ann and I can follow such a lifestyle, but neither of us feel guilty about taking the occasional holiday or having a meal in a cosy restaurant – nor should we.

Our dues are always paid on time, the odd 'bob' or two are given to charity, plus we are ever available to family and friends; so with all this in mind, why should we not cosset ourselves a little?

However, when self-indulgence, to any degree, is detrimental to others – that is a different matter. In this direction, parents giving their offspring absurd names comes to mind.

So called 'celebrities' are often guilty of this; perhaps they feel the bestowing of bizarre soubriquets adds to their own prominence, they working on the maxim that there is no such thing as bad publicity.

Now, if they wish to change their own forenames to something daft, it's up to them, but to so afflict their children is little short of abuse; for it is the unfortunate minor who will have to go through life enduring mockery regarding their monikers.

Mind you, it is not only those in the public eye who are culpable, as a cursory glance at the names listed beneath group photos in local newspapers confirm; it is easy to laugh at such, but that's the folly of it – mirth at the expense of an innocent youngster.

Still, whilst this is thoughtless and unfair, there are other ways parents, arguably, pursue selfish interests which can inflict far more trauma and misery on their progeny than the bestowing of a silly name; it can lie in the excessive 'pushing' of a son or daughter which goes well beyond enthusiastic and supportive encouragement.

To be fair, they might well say – and, indeed, believe – that their sole motivation is to forward the interests of their loved ones, but so often the reality lies in a father or mother attempting to fulfill their own ambitions – dreams, even – through a child, with little regard for the youngster's own wishes.

A boy or a girl, good at a particular sport, or with musical, dancing, acting, artistic talent and the like, can be driven almost ruthlessly in pursuit of excellence; they can be dominated, even bullied; the upshot of this, often, is that the gifted young person will eventually rebel and turn their back upon their special flair; thus a talent is lost for all time, and the world – plus the hapless young person – is the ultimate loser.

It can be even worse – lives can be distorted, even wrecked, when unfair, sometimes oppressive assumptions are laid upon young shoulders. Parents who expect son or daughter to go to university, then adopt a profession which might, in its wake, bring kudos to the older pair; or to enter the family business in order solely to ensure the continuity of the clan in terms of running the firm.

Such folk are all too often indulging blatant self-aggrandisement, their aspiration being, in effect, to feed personal ambition rather than, at heart, desiring the fulfillment and happiness of their offspring.

All young people should be encouraged to gain a sound education but, once completed, they must be free to pursue their own ambitions and dreams – though clearly it is vital they are able to make a living.

I was most fortunate in my own parents; for although farming had been in our family for generations, my two brothers and myself were at total liberty to choose our paths.

My respect for, and gratitude to them, is immense; no self-indulgence there – just love.

39

Words

*T*HERE is a strange, at times, absurd contradiction in my character which so often causes me to be tolerant of major follies perpetrated by institutions and people, whilst railing against the relative – at times, the exceedingly – trivial.

In no direction does this intolerance manifest itself more than in the use of words. If someone came on television or radio and voiced an opinion on some political or national issue with which I disagreed, I would naturally accept their right to views very different from my own – as long as the statement is prefaced with 'Hello', 'Good evening' or, indeed, nothing at all. However, if the utterance began with that dire, but widespread greeting, 'Hi', then within me any dissent – or, indeed even agreement – regarding the viewpoint expressed would be overwhelmed by outrage at the use of that lazy Americanism.

Folk come on TV as contestants on quiz shows and the like. If when introduced, they say 'Hi', curmudgeon that I am, I hope that they get every question wrong. But I do root for them if they use civilised British terms. Petty? Small minded? Of course it is – but such is the nature of irrational prejudice.

Then there is the ever increasing use of an annoying, and highly inaccurate word when one asks after the well-being of an acquaintance or friend; 'How are you?' – the enquiry; 'Good' – the reply. Now if you were investigating a person's character, then such an answer could well be fair and accurate, but if seeking to know the state of somebody's health, then, if it's positive, 'Well' would be a suitable riposte, if the opposite, then there are a range of words and expressions which would suffice.

Annoying also, to me, is the grievous over use – even abuse – of 'Cheers'. Not that long ago, it was principally invoked when raising a glass – an expression of good will to others. Now, though, it flows incessantly through life covering multitudinous circumstances. It can be a word of greeting – or, indeed, farewell, or an expression of thanks. Used in introduction other than 'Hello', or, in ironic tones, it can represent mild anger or disillusionment. It's individual choice, of course, but we British, being the possessors of a rich, varied, evocative language, should employ it. Suitable alternatives to this so hackneyed term are manifold.

'Guys', too, brings forth vituperation from this moaning old toad. The dictionary states the word means, 'A man or boy'; possibly it derives from the famous seventeenth century terrorist of that forename – one Mr Fawkes. For certain, though, it refers to the male of the species. Now, though, often it is used for females also. Why this has developed is a mystery, but surely when there are such a fine array of words available to differentiate between genders, it should cease.

Then there is 'Cool'. These days it is employed in manifold ways, and there are some folk (usually of a younger generation) who use it incessantly in reaction to the widest gamut of situations and news. It is employed to express satisfaction, gratitude, admiration, agreement – even mild disillusion and disappointment. Whilst 'cool' does not offend this pedantic moaner to the same degree as does use of the two letter abomination imported from the Yanks, surely it is a shame that what is basically an indicator of temperature, climate and so forth, is used in place of that rich array of verbiage adorning our mother tongue which would be infinitely more suitable. Perhaps the allure of the word is, simply, its brevity – so swift to speak, even easier to text.

There are numerous other expressions which annoy, but to be fair, this serial old grumbler needs, now and again, to look at his own failings, which are manifold – including the use of annoying words and expressions. 'Not many of us left', I hear myself say – plain daft when one considers that world population is rocketing. The use of the lazy 'Eh?' instead of 'I beg your pardon?' and, all too regularly (especially when seeing the football results) that of a six letter expletive beginning with 'B' – plus multitudes more.

Hypocrite that I am, though, it'll not stop me finding fault with others – at great length.

40

The Broom

*U*NLIKE 'Trigger' of *Only Fools and Horses* fame, whose council broom had been updated over the years with four new heads and three replacement handles, ours – bought as a full, working unit – swept our paths and patio for over two decades without maintenance.

Its quality was top class, mind you – I was in the trade at the time so was able, cheaply, to obtain the best – but its longevity was still remarkable, even allowing for the fact I possibly never used it as often as I should have, and when I did, it was never with enthusiasm. However, a few weeks ago it went into speedy decline. The main problem was that it became seriously 'follically' challenged; tufts of the orange hued bristle began to fall out alarmingly quickly.

In little over a week it was possessing of less bristle than even myself. Though a man of serial indecision, I knew action was required in the very short term. Rapidly this was upgraded to immediately, as Ann noticed a serious development which I really should have seen much earlier, it being a major cause of the loss of the brightly coloured 'foliage'; it was riddled with woodworm. Instantly the broom was sentenced to the quarantine which is a dustbin and it was decided I would purchase a replacement the following morning when I went to get a paper.

'I'll not be long,' I said to Ann as I set off – a statement of ill-founded optimism, or so it turned out. Leaving the newsagents, which supplied my needs instantly, I headed to a store with agricultural connections, which would stock brooms – surely. The young gent behind the counter was confident they did, pointing me in the general direction where he said they would be found. The hunt began; there was no sign of bristled appliances in the area I was sent – thus I sought further advice. A lady, certain she knew the location kindly led me to the opposite end of the store; she stopped suddenly, clearly nonplussed. 'This is where they are usually,' said she. If this was the case, then clearly they had, like tadpoles, developed legs and escaped, for the display before us was of wellington boots. The help of another member of staff was sought; he confessed he was unsure of their site, but willingly joined in the search. After a meander to the far corners of the showroom, he raised his voice in triumph – 'here they are.' He was justified, technically, in using the plural – there were two broom heads (though not a handle in site) lying on top of a tallish unit.

I thanked all for their efforts, quickly selected the smaller of the two (which seemed ideal for our purposes) then enquired, not unreasonably, where one would find the shaft. There seemed puzzlement over my request, as if it was customary to sell heads on their own; perhaps one was expected to get on hands and knees to use it. The original assistant intervened, he knew where they were, accurately;

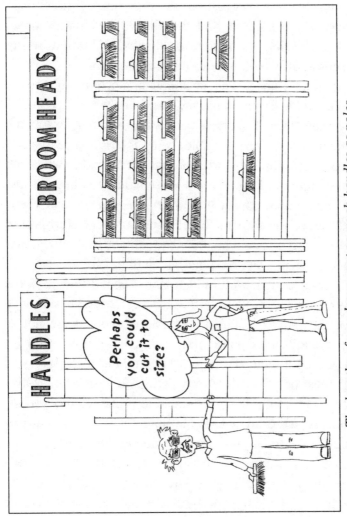

The lengths of wood were not so much handles as poles. . .

143

there were three. Problem solved? Sadly no; the head required a screw-in handle – none were remotely as sophisticated. A suggestion as to a nearby (tolerably) venue where I might find the elusive brush was made, most helpfully, so muttering thanks, I hurtled in its direction; only half an hour had been wasted.

At first glance, this spacious emporium seemed to provide a happy ending to the quest, for within seconds, I saw a selection of likely heads – well, four to be exact; one of them looked very suitable, being the right size at a fair price. I seized it, then gazed around for a handle (why such crucial pieces of wood are sold separately is beyond me, but such would appear the norm); no sign of any. A lady with the company name emblazoned on her t-shirt passed by. Instantly I sought her help and she obliged with similar alacrity. 'This way,' was her instruction; I followed.

In a far corner, well hidden from general view, stood a pile of – in theory – apt staffs. Just a cursory glance though brought dismay; for these lengths of wood were not so much handles as poles; they could have been used for propelling a punt. 'Perhaps you could cut it to size,' said this most helpful lady. A city and guilds carpenter, with a saw bench might have been able to – just; chances of me doing so were nil. I left; the hunt for this cleaning tool would have to be postponed to another day.

It was – the next to be exact; for there we were in a supermarket searching for kitchen towels when we were confronted with light-weight brooms (with handles), on special offer. Our paths are passable once more.

41

Traffic Jams

*I*N previous meanderings, I have admitted to being the unwilling possessor of the fault of chronic impatience.

As I get even older, I am aware it is a blemish which becomes ever more vivid. Indeed, it is in danger of becoming to myself as much a curse as a deplorable defect in character.

Increasingly I find myself behaving almost irrationally if I am kept waiting for even the shortest time. If in a restaurant, anything longer than a ten minute delay in receiving food makes me feel like walking out, going home and having bread and cheese. As almost invariably I'll be in company, it is not something I do, but the desire will be with me nonetheless.

Mind you, some eating establishments give fair warning – 'As all our food is freshly cooked, there can, at busy times, be a delay in serving the meal.' My experience is that it is not just at peak times; however, at least an alarm has been sounded. Personally, if I see such a sign then I'm off. Mind you, it could be the establishment is victimised by its own honesty, for you can go to places with no such

145

warning and still wait so long that malnutrition sets in. In truth I'll settle for a pasty warmed in a microwave rather than loiter. Still, nightmare though I am in this, I'm even worse when behind the wheel. Not that I lack respect for others or expect always to be hurtling along at a merry pace – but I do desire motion, even if traffic dictates it is slow.

Thus agitation requiring from me instant action occurs when, on the highway, all vehicle movement ceases and transport powered by the 'infernal' combustion engine stretches stationary, to the far horizon. It happened recently when travelling across Roborough Down heading for the great 'Ocean City'.

What caught my eye, some two hundred yards ahead, was a large van painted in vivid pink. It was not moving, nor was the traffic between me and it, or that which stretched ahead to the brow of a hill some half mile away.

Roadworks? Worse still, an accident? Who knows? For certain my incurable intolerance of sitting in a queue took hold immediately.

I had no urgent appointment in Plymouth – it would not have mattered if the journey had taken double its normal time. Such logic played no part; directly opposite where I was stopped was a narrow road (which I knew would get even narrower).

To me it was akin to espying a lifeboat when aboard a sinking ship. Instantly I steered into the lane – and hoped for the best. Having possibly greater knowledge of the by-ways of the area than the main roads, I knew there was a route, circuitous true, which would deliver me to Crownhill – thus, hopefully, avoiding the jams.

I drove past a well known hotel, then trundled down to, and through, Milton Combe (not the widest of highways, these, but mercifully virtually traffic free).

Past that village there is a lane which leads eventually to Tamerton Foliot – so, in effect, the city. I took it, as I knew the fact there was grass growing down the middle meant that probably just a couple of cars used it in a week. Now I could possibly have been right about this, but unfortunately the other motor, which was part of the theory, was doing so at the same time as myself; for some quarter of a mile along it, I was confronted by a Range Rover.

Fortunately the driver was a true gentleman and seeing my decrepit state, reversed at an impressive pace to a passing place at least half a mile back. I thanked him; time had been swallowed, but not too much. Intrepidly I soldiered on.

Around the next bend, I encountered a mounted sturdy black horse, going very slowly the same way, looking so old its previous owner could have been Dick Turpin. It was a while before I could progress.

Having done so, I was confronted by the gas board doing repairs, then likewise the Highways Agency and finally, a tractor and trailer going frustratingly slowly.

Eventually, Crownhill – and the pink van was even further ahead! A lesson learned? Sadly I doubt it!

42

Personal Qualities

*J*OHN F. Kennedy, when musing on the qualities a person needs in life to be revered in death, posed questions he felt would be aired by historians in later years; 'Did the man (or woman) have integrity, did the man have unselfishness, did the man have courage, did the man have consistency?' All are most admirable. Indeed, anyone possessing of the four would be exceptional, for so many folk – even great, iconic ones – are, or were, lacking in some.

Winston Churchill assuredly was inconsistent as in his political life he twice 'crossed the floor' of the House of Commons to change party allegiances, whilst in his personal life he could be selfish. Also possession of some of these attributes does not guarantee anyone is of high character. After all, Adolf Hitler did not lack courage, being decorated for valour in the Great War, whilst his gaining of power in Germany owed much to relentless, bold consistency. Conversely, President Kennedy, himself, was far from flawless – his personal life clearly, at times, lacking integrity.

Mind you, it is not only the eminent, 'The Great and the

Good' (of whom primarily the President was referring) who can be possessed of such virtues. Many a man or woman, who have enjoyed no overt success or prominence in life, will depart this world admired, respected – long remembered – for their contribution to those around them. Such good people will possess some of the qualities listed by J.F.K. plus, often, others; for there are myriad attributes which can, if integral to someone's character, elevate he or she towards nobility, ensuring they will be valued by their peers. Active compassion – empathy with those less fortunate, plus a will to help them. Loyalty to another, not blind or blinkered, but of a kind which supports those unfairly treated – even oppressed – by those about them. Also tolerance is a fine trait – as long as it is not acceptance of the criminal or anti-social.

The recognition of the rights of others to have different beliefs and lifestyles to one's own can be hard; thus those who without question respect such, who recognise the freedom of individuals to conduct their affairs in, at times, eccentric fashion (as long as they remain within the law), are to be admired. Sadly there are far too many in our society lacking this forbearance.

Generosity of spirit, too, is to be treasured – basic goodwill towards, and trust in others. Also, crucially, an unquestioning acceptance of the fallibility of the human race (including, of course, oneself) plus a reluctance to suspect conspiracy, dishonesty and duplicity in people unless there exists clear evidence of its presence.

Then there is courtesy – of all positive mannerisms, this surely is the easiest to cultivate. It requires no compromise, no pursuit of ethics, no gallantry or defiance

– it merely entails the observation of a seemly, gentle code of behaviour, of thought and consideration for others, and the awareness we share this crowded world with so many. The understanding that politeness, grace and a civilised demeanour are crucial individual facets are essential if boorishness, disorder, even anarchy are to be avoided; And cannot courtesy feed and elevate the spirits of the giver as effectively as those of the receiver?

There is a further virtue – assuredly not possessed by myself – which is to be both admired and prized; Patience. So much which is good is encompassed within it – perseverance, tenacity, equanimity, understanding, even sufferance. Those imbued with some of these qualities, who are accepting of the foibles, idiosyncrasies, even selfishness of many with whom they come into contact, and are able to make allowance for such failings are to be revered – perhaps envied as well. For understanding of the way others conduct their lives often means they are able to get on with their own.

No human being will possess limitless qualities – a number, sadly, will have few. There will, though, amongst rich and poor, the famed and the relatively obscure, the front runners and those to the rear, be a sprinkling of human beings who enrich the existence of those about them. They are, and, when they pass on, will be, remembered as ladies and gentlemen in the finest sense of the word.

43

Enemies Of...

A MAJOR development of recent years has been the rise of groups calling themselves, 'Friends of'. So many art centres, theatres, churches, charities, sports clubs, doctor's surgeries, community projects and the like, are aided in both financial and practical ways by bodies of men and women giving freely of their time and energies, and sometimes their own money as well. Without the dedication and generosity of such folk, so many valued local organisations would struggle greatly – some might well fail entirely. My respect and admiration for those good people is immense – thank heavens for them.

Having said this, I am not, never have been, nor ever will be a member of such an altruistic band; I am much too lacking in energy, commitment, enthusiasm and magnanimity to get involved with any society of benefactors, no matter how good the cause. Sadly I have to concede that if ever I did feel inspired to champion anything worthy, such nobility would be drowned by a tsunami of apathy.

However, my somewhat perverse mind and nature brings me, increasingly, to the notion that perhaps it is

151

time to create alliances of negativity recruited from those who object to unacceptable behavioural deficits in others. Is it not time to start movements which oppose unwelcome, unsavoury aspects of human nature and the world in which we dwell? Such could be entitled 'Enemies of. . .' – they would not be few.

There should be mobilisation against a plethora of transgressors who have scant respect for the rights, welfare and quality of life of their fellow citizens. Litter louts, who pollute our streets and public places; even worse, those who allow their dogs to foul footways then do not deign to pick it up; pests who hurtle along streets, often beyond the speed limit, blaring raucous music through open windows; likewise builders on site working with their radios amplified to a decibel level which would disturb the peace a mile away; idiots who use spray cans to deface buildings, and worse still, malicious vandals who destroy public property and amenities.

Barricades should be manned also (metaphorically) against the selfish, thoughtless, arrogant people – all too numerous – who pursue personal goals and ambitions, usually of an outdoor nature and often hazardous, without the necessary skills, guile and equipment to achieve them. Too often brave men and women – frequently in a voluntary capacity – have to put themselves in danger to effect a rescue: A lifeboat crew having to turn out in rough seas to rescue a yachtsman (and it's usually male) who has set out severely ill-equipped in terms of both apparatus and knowledge. The likes of the valiant Dartmoor Rescue Group (and, in some parts of the land, members of Mountain Rescue) risking 'life and limb' to assist mindless fools who ignore warnings of bad weather and take to the potentially perilous upland terrain devoid, again, of the correct gear plus lacking awareness of the calamities which could engulf them.

Then there are those who swim in heavy seas and dangerous currents when advised not to – who surf in conditions with which they do not have the competence to cope – thus lifeguards have to put themselves in harm's way to save them.

Should we not also be intolerant of those in shops or public places who are rude, discourteous, at times, downright abusive. Of those who regularly cause trouble largely because they are unable to hold their liquor. Irksome as well (to me at least) are folk and societies who collect for charity but cannot accept that not everyone is sympathetic to their cause; at times they pester – even harass – people due to their excessive, self justifying zeal. Also, I feel, men and women who write to newspapers, letters for publication critical of others, yet ask that their names be not printed – craven, to say the least.

What, though, can adversaries do regarding these ignorant individuals who behave in the aforementioned (and numerous other) hostile, selfish ways? It's not easy, clearly, to remedy matters, but possibly two courses of action can be pursued: Where the law is broken, the miscreants must be charged; where accepted civilised standards are ignored, perpetrators should expect no tolerance from their fellow citizens. Will this happen? Sadly it's doubtful.

44

Poets & Poetry

MY approach to poetry is akin to my position on music – I don't know that much about either, but, generally speaking, modern rarely appeals. However, I am aware of that which I enjoy – often very much – from all eras and in both fields.

Some years ago, the BBC commissioned a poll to ascertain the nation's 'favourite' poems, publishing, in accordance with the survey's findings, a book in which were printed the top one hundred. Assuredly they were a most eclectic collection containing works which would satisfy most tastes, including mine.

The most popular, by a considerable margin, was a poem of Rudyard Kipling. Probably few bards ever penned in the English language as many well known and recited odes as did he, but assuredly his most famous, popular and quoted is the penetrating, rhythmic *If*. Some folk classed it as being 'jingoistic', a judgement which baffles, for it has nothing to do with nationhood or chauvinism, rather it is a view of the qualities a person requires to be, as he states in the final line, 'A man, my son' (or, clearly, 'A woman, my daughter', as there is not a single attribute stated which is exclusively male). The most perceptive line in this fine elegy? A matter of opinion, naturally, but to me it is the suggestion that to a just, fair minded person, 'All men (women) count with you, but none too much'. Was ever there a more egalitarian exhortation than this?

The charismatic Dylan Thomas also features amongst the anthology – no surprise, of course, as the Welshman, who died before he was forty, has to be amongst the finest poets this nation has ever produced. It is arguable he created nothing more moving or emotive than those riveting words entreating his Father, terminally ill, to defy the end, inevitable though it was – 'Do not go gentle into that good night; Old age should burn and rave at close of day – rage, rage against the dying of the light.' These words when read linger long in the mind. When heard spoken by Thomas himself – an ancient recording in his mesmeric Welsh tones – they can almost chill the blood.

As indeed can the works of Wilfred Owen, written in the trenches during that devilish conflict, The Great War. So much riveting, disturbing writing came from him that it is not easy to choose the best, but is it not fair to say none is better than, *Anthem for Doomed Youth*, amongst the lines of which, the soldier poet (himself doomed) drafts the despairingly evocative words describing the butchery – 'The shrill demented choirs of wailing shells.'

Those who survived the carnage, when returning home, would have been in need of tranquillity and beauty. If walking in England's 'Green and Pleasant Land' it could be some inner peace would be theirs if they were able to come upon William Wordsworth's, 'Host of Golden

Daffodils'. If they did, possibly they might heed the perceptive words of William Henry Davies, 'What is this life if full or care, we have no time to stand and stare.' Far too few of us in this day and age take notice of these insightful words.

Being an island race, we Britons possess an affinity to the oceans, and clearly appreciate the flowing lines of such as John Masefield's, 'I must go down to the sea, again, to the lonely sea and the sky' and the like. Also we are a patriotic people and thus have empathy with those inspiring words in *The Soldier* by Rupert Brooke – 'If I should die, think only this of me – that there is some corner of a foreign field that is forever England.' War, sacrifice and death feature prominently in this absorbing collection with most folk in the poll leaning towards the serious.

There are, though, some lighthearted choices such as John Betjeman's witty, *Diary of a Church Mouse*, and Edward Lear's, *The Owl and the Pussycat*. Also, thankfully, there is love, such as in Shakespeare's sonnets, and Elizabeth Barrett Browning's enchanting 'How do I love thee? Let me count the ways.'

On the whole, however, we British take our poetry as it is said we take our pleasures – seriously. My own favourite from these and the manifold others that I would mention if space permitted? Possibly Thomas's exhortation, in the face of death, to fight. Being an old man, this appeals, even though, ultimately, it will be doomed to failure – though not too soon I hope.

45

A Restful Day

*F*OLLOWING a busy week, Saturday's dawning was welcome.

A glance out the window on this autumn day took in overcast skies with drizzle; excellent – too wet for gardening. Spirits were lifted further – Argyle were away; thus no angst laden trip to Home Park after lunch. Granted there would be stress when scores came along – but that which cannot be avoided must be endured. Thus as we sat at breakfast, Ann and me, a peaceful, relaxing day was anticipated.

The 'best laid plans', however, started to unravel immediately. Halfway through my cornflakes, the phone rang. Having watched recently repeats of *Keeping up Appearances*, where that appalling social climber, 'Hyacinth Bouquet', always hurtles to answer the phone 'as it might be someone important', promptly I dropped my spoon, rushed to the hallway then lifted the receiver. Was it a vital call? No. Was it an annoying one? Exceedingly so. A gent with a foreign accent suggested he should send someone to upgrade our computer. I informed him that in our house he had as much chance of finding the Holy Grail as he did any such technical appliance, thanked him for his call, and returned to my repast. Halfway through munching on a piece of toast, Alexander Graham Bell's infernal creation trilled again. There was a lady on the line this time. She came rapidly to the point – 'Was I still on the council?' (not an infrequent question), because if I was she wished to report that not for the first time, her next door neighbour had been playing music – loudly – into the early hours, and so wanted something done about it. I sympathised, but told her my days in public office were but a memory; I did, though, supply the numbers of a couple of current councillors (I keep a list by the phone for such eventualities) suggesting she contact them.

Breakfast was completed without further interruption, but just as we arose from the table that menace of communication sounded once more. The will to live was beginning to weaken, but valiantly I picked up the receiver; my spirits hurtled skywards – it was for Ann. Unfortunately, hers went in the opposite direction for at the other end was a lady who can 'talk for England'. Feeling guilty I gave her the appliance, then escaped down town to buy a paper. Sadly she remained the victim of an ear bashing when I returned. Eventually she was able to end this audio assault, and slumped wearily into an easy chair to sip the strong coffee we both needed.

A minimal amount only had been consumed before further discordant chimes came from the hall; a touch different this one – the front door bell. Stood on the step were a lady and gent keen to save our souls – representatives of a well known religious sect who appear to spend

The 'best laid plans', however, started to unravel immediately.

159

much of their lives calling on folk, in the name of 'The Lord'. We had a civilised conversation but I did not encourage them to call again; they will. Just as they left, the post lady arrived, depositing five letters. Following the swallowing of tepid coffee, they were opened – four 'junk mail' the other a bill; the day was not improving.

There was a further burst from the phone just before lunch; Ann answered this time and told the caller we were fully double glazed right down to the cat flap. Our meal went uninterrupted – almost; half way through a third cup of tea the bullying receiver demanded lifting once more. This time it sounded like a Dalek on the line; in terrifying staccato tones I was told our gas meter needed reading; unnerved by that voice, I obeyed immediately.

Two more calls came that afternoon – one suggesting I invest in a world cruise, the other convinced ours was the number of the animal rescue centre. There were also live visitors; two smartly dressed gents, with American accents, stood on the doorstep – Mormons. Clearly my soul is under dire threat as, twice in one day, there were those trying to save it. These fellows had no chance; if my inner self needs rescuing, it's not going to be put in the hands of 'Yanks'.

Did the day improve? No – Argyle lost. Roll on Monday, work – and peace.

46

Theft

CHAMBERS Dictionary defines 'Steal' as meaning, 'To take by theft, especially secretly.' This covers the most widely used – and understood – meaning of the word; The obtaining, illicitly, of tangible objects and goods, or money, to which one has no right or claim unless one purchases them.

Relatively few folk do this – probably for two reasons. Usually conscience will not allow such, but secondly, if moral character is insufficiently sturdy, fear of having one's 'collar felt' can be most effective. For such stealing as this is a criminal act which can lead to a prison sentence.

There are, though, many other forms of it which although causing distress and loss, will not land the perpetrators before a judge and jury. For instance, someone employs a builder to work on their house, the job is completed satisfactorily, but the householder fails to pay what is due. He or she will have reaped the benefits from a tradesman's time and skills, possibly will have left the craftsman to supply materials also, yet will have put this ill-used fellow seriously – perhaps even calamitously – out of pocket. Is this not theft? By any moral standards, it clearly is – but it does not break the criminal law, though it really is time it did – many are forced into the misery of bankruptcy as a result of such.

Then there is lack of punctuality. It is said that, 'Procrastination is the thief of time', but to this highly impatient scribe, who values every minute, every second (as I get older inevitably they get fewer), anybody who keeps people waiting without good excuse are embezzlers, illicitly taking from them something vital. An over-reaction? Possibly – but I feel intensely that the purloining of a person's time is almost as unacceptable as the taking illegally of their property. Some people, though, appear to do such with impunity, with arrogance; serial time-bandits, uncaring that their selfish indulgence can cause inconvenience, possibly distress – even harm – to others. Many too are hypocritical in that whilst they are cavalier regarding others' time, they zealously value their own.

However, whilst the above are, to me, examples of, at best, unacceptable selfishness, at worst, sheer criminality, there is a further act of theft – seemingly ever more prevalent – which could be said to be the nastiest and most destructive of all. Shakespeare certainly thought as much, for he wrote, regarding the malevolent, vindictive destruction of a person's reputation, 'who steals my purse steals trash; 'Tis something, 'tis nothing. 'Twas mine, 'tis his and has been slave to thousands; But he that filches from me my good name robs me of that which not enriches him and makes me poor indeed.'

The spreading of rumour, innuendo or, so often, blatant

lies, has existed since the dawn of history – folk recklessly, often malignly impugning the reputation of others. Clearly the 'Bard of Avon' was aware of such over 400 years ago – hence his insightful prose.

Sometimes the 'filching' of a 'good name' can be laid at the door of ignorance or intolerance rather than deliberate trouble-making. Someone a touch eccentric, idiosyncratic or of a solitary, exceedingly private nature (given, increasingly, the mischievously damning description of being a 'loner') can, just because they are unconventional, be the target of unpleasant, at times even vicious vilification from others in the community. Some of these verbal abusers will not intend harm – though they can assuredly cause such. Others clearly do, and bring misery to the innocent.

Until recent times, victims of such piracy regarding their reputation could seek some redress within the law, inadequate and expensive though such action could be; for the malign bullies attacking the reputations of decent people could be sued in court if libelled by the written media or slandered by word of mouth. This remains the case regarding traditional means of communication. The winning of such cases – though never easy – would go some way towards restoring a 'good name', and provide some monetary compensation for the misery caused. However, it is virtually impossible for victims to defend themselves if targeted on social media; such cruel attacks against the famous – and less known – abound with reputations often destroyed by the spreading of lies. I know not what can be done – but it really is time the innocent were protected, the vindictive and bullies exposed and disgraced.

47

A Lack of Moss

*T*HE dictionary describes adage as 'an old saying that has been popularly accepted as truth'.

Now, that this is accurate concerning all ancient homilies, I doubt, but assuredly I have learned the hard way, and to my cost, that it is brutally pertinent when it comes to a long lasting defect in my character and behaviour – 'A rolling stone gathers no moss.'

This refers, of course, to the 'foliage' which bears upon it the Queen's head; due to a lifelong, totally mistaken belief that 'the other man's grass is greener' and, despite evidence in abundance it's not, I've been a serial wanderer work-wise.

In recent years I have been somewhat more constant, this largely dictated by advancing (indeed, advanced) years and an appalling lack of skill, knowledge and ability when it comes to mastering modern technology (though, to be fair, I wasn't much good at the old, either).

I left school with no idea of what I wanted to do. Looking back, being of an indolent, unambitious nature – and not blessed with self-discipline – it could have been predicted that I would not approach the working world with the right attitude. I was well aware that, my mouth being 'silver spoonless', I would have to work for a living but from early on I pursued jobs rather than a career, seeing employment as the means by which food was put on the table – and liquor in the glass – rather than also being a major source of fulfilment. Strangely, a working life which at present has spanned almost 60 years, started, and will no doubt finish (not too soon, I hope), working for the *Tavistock Times Gazette*.

Back in 1959 on leaving school, I went to this venerable local paper as a junior reporter – though then it was the *Times*, the other half to the present title being a separate publication (indeed, the town's first, founded in 1857). I lasted but a few months. Then, as now, I enjoyed writing but having to stick to facts (a crucial requirement of journalism) was beyond me. Some years later – the late 70s – I worked for the *Gazette*, mainly on advertising, with some writing thrown in, then left to open a shop in the town – a somewhat unsuccessful venture as so many of my 'customers' came in to grumble about the council (me being a member) rather than to buy.

In the early 1990s, good folk, with mercifully short memories, allowed me to return to our local paper, where I have remained ever since – albeit on a part time basis, thus in other employments as well. So there have been virtually six decades of, often, daft wanderlust in terms of earning a living.

For a little while in my early days, I worked with my parents on the farm; whilst I have no doubt being a large landowner, steering a Range Rover around the estate with

165

others doing the work, would have been a great life, to actually have to fight the land and weather to make a living is very different; there might be harder ways than farming to earn a crust, but I can't think of any.

Mind you, being a door-to-door salesman (which I was – for several years) was no sinecure; self-employed, working entirely on commission, the mind was perpetually concentrated; still, I rather enjoyed it – and it provided a rich seam of experiences, some hilarious; likewise the couple of years I spent as an insurance agent.

A summer spent as a security guard in a holiday camp and another driving an ice cream van were similarly eventful. More conventional occupation came my way as a full time firefighter – also a few years in our splendid local retained service – a few months as a civil servant in London, a spell employed in a local office and several months working nights in an aircraft factory in Bristol (so under employed, I kept awake by writing my first novel). There were others, too, which lasted just a few days, possibly the daftest of which was attempting to sell encyclopaedias to American Servicemen in Germany.

So, looking back at this chequered labouring life, am I able to trumpet the words of Edith Piaf's vibrant song – 'No Regrets'? No, decidedly not; a touch more foresight and 'stickability' on my part would have given far more security to my dear wife, Ann, and our sons. Yet there has been a small personal plus; riding this roller-coaster has meant rarely being bored, plus, for a man of no imagination and no desire to do research – an abundance of materials with which to write tales.

48

The Table

WE needed a new kitchen table – even I could see that. Though, in truth a man whose awareness of furniture goes little beyond a chair to sit in of an evening, a decent sized television to watch and a comfortable bed in which to lay my weary body at night (though being something of an insomniac, I spend many a darkened hour just laying there hearing the hall clock chiming the quarters), I had not the slightest doubt the table needed replacing. Not that there was anything wrong with it in terms of quality; the opposite, in fact, for it was well made and quite pleasing to the eye. The problem was it was too big – a round table which would have accommodated most of King Arthur's knights; this was no major minus when the family were growing up, but they having long since gone out into the world, Ann and I, when sitting on opposite sides of it, had almost to signal to each other in semaphore to make contact.

So the decision was made, long ago, that it had to be replaced; easier said than done, however, for finding a neat circular piece of modest size and – crucially – with one central pillar rather than four legs (a monumental minus in the existing one, as each leg appeared to be positioned in such a way that sliding a chair past was an art), and at the right price, was almost akin to searching for the Holy Grail. In reality, it went on for years – though not continuously, more when the spirit moved us (which was very rarely in my case).

Then, on a Saturday a few months back, came the 'eureka' moment. Ann, along with her sister, Margaret, took the excellent community bus for a day out in Exeter. She returned late afternoon in elevated spirits (the opposite to mine as just before she got home I heard the final league football results of the season – Argyle had lost and, in consequence, had missed out on the play-offs). My passing on of this tragic news did nothing to dampen her spirits, though, for she had enjoyed a triumphant day; she had found, and bought, a table – one perfect for the limited space in our kitchen. It was to be delivered the following weekend – the countdown had begun.

Ann had been told that on the Friday evening we would receive a phone call from the store which would give us a two hour time slot for the following day during which the new acquisition would be delivered. On Tuesday evening the phone rang in the middle of *Midsomer Murders* – annoyingly. On answering it, I was confronted by dialogue far more petrifying than anything I had been watching on TV; a disembodied female voice informed me in chilling, staccato tones, that our order would be brought to us the following Saturday some time between 7.30 and 14.30 hours – and that we would be contacted again. We hoped we would, for this was hardly the two hour slot promised.

The good lady was true to her word, for the next evening

the phone went again at exactly the same time giving the same message – and again the next. On the Friday, though, the communication was different; this remarkably hard working woman informed that our delivery would arrive the next morning, between 10.30 and 12.30; the van driver would make contact half an hour before. The call came at 11.30 – our 'prize' would appear at 'high noon'.

Impressively, at the stroke of mid-day a van drew up. I opened the door and awaited the coming of a pristine table; suddenly I was seized by a potent mix of terror and despair, as coming down the path were a brace of gents each carrying a cardboard box. Only a naive idiot such as myself could not have foreseen we were to be attacked by the ogre that is flat-packs. The boxes were deposited in our kitchen, trance-like I signed for them (upon a modern monstrosity, with a 'stick' for a pen) and wished these fellows 'good day'. Sadly it was not to be such for us.

We managed, with much difficulty, to extract the parts of the glass creation from their containers; it became clear why the chaps had staggered down the path – granite could not have weighed more. Mercifully Ann was able to follow the terse instructions.

Following a traumatic hour of wrestling with the beast, a stylish glass table evolved. There was though, a small drawback – it wobbled like a jelly. Help was needed; thus a call to our good, practical son James who lives nearby. Like an able doctor, he diagnosed the malady, and having modern tools – plus, crucially, the skill to use them – cured it – the structure is now wobble free. And flat packs? Surely the creation of the devil; after all, if I buy a new shirt, I'm not expected to sew on the sleeves.

h

49

Heroes

MOST of us in our lives have a hero – or heroes – men and women for whom we have admiration, esteem, even devotion. It can last a lifetime; people who capture one's imagination, who bring enchantment, excitement, to an often mundane world. I only ever had one – a legendary sportsman whose fame was mammoth when I was born (even though the war was on), remaining so for the rest of a long, dazzling career; indeed, a household name still, even though he died some 20 years ago. His name? I'll come to that later.

Now, whilst this gent is the only one I view with wonder – with reverence – there are many other folk of both sexes for whom I have huge regard, an esteem which I will never lose. Always I have been interested in politics – even as a boy – but have been fortunate in that I've been spared the affliction of dogma and unyielding party loyalty. The political figures I admire come from across the 'political divide' regarding our country, whilst there are foreign leaders, and sportsmen, of whom, also, I have much regard – sadly, virtually all now dead. Sir Winston Churchill, naturally, is well to the fore in the list of greats; his inspired leadership of the nation – the Free World, in fact – during the war will be talked of for generations to come.

The man whom I honour most in British public life however, is far less known – Ernest Bevin. He was a member of the immediate post war government, and often classed as the finest foreign secretary to represent the affairs of these islands during the twentieth century. Born and bred on the Devon/Somerset border, the son of poor parents, he was orphaned at the age of six, and left school to go to work aged nine. With such a hideously disadvantaged start in life, his accomplishments are surely monumental. His Prime Minister, also – to me – was one of the outstanding figures of the past 100 years; Clement Attlee was a principled, honourable and able man; arguably the finest peacetime British leader of that century.

The only one, I believe, remotely in his league, was Margaret Thatcher; an honest politician who usually stuck to the policies stated in her party's manifesto, she has ever received – even after death – more censure, at times vilification, than was her due. Was her gender a factor in this? In what, deplorably, remains an age in which women so often struggle to get a fair deal, it is a strong possibility. After all, is it not odd that, in the protracted history of the House of Commons there has only ever been one solitary Speaker from the female side – the admirable Betty Boothroyd, whom many would say was the finest of modern times. Disappointingly, on the world stage, whilst there have been numerous ladies who have done so much, selflessly, for those about them, few have come to prominence.

This applies clearly to the 'Florence Nightingales' who go unrewarded and often unthanked, to minister to the sick in the 'Third World', putting themselves in harm's way, receiving little or no tangible reward. Generally they remain anonymous, but my regard for them is vast.

Likewise for some highly significant figures beyond our shores. The charismatic – and valiant – Martin Luther King, who by virtue of his mastery of the English language, his force of personality, his steadfast adherence to a policy of non-violence, brought at least a semblance of civil liberties to the black people of the United States. There was, too, Nelson Mandela – truly a giant of his times; serving almost 30 years in a South African prison because of his unrelenting opposition to apartheid; when he was released he emerged with no bitterness; as president he preached only forgiveness and unity.

A man of bravery, also, was he who ended the 'Cold War' – Mikhail Gorbachev; we sleep easier in our beds because of him, despite the coming of Putin.

Back, though, to the beginning of this diatribe – my life-long hero. This is (in my view) the greatest footballer who ever breathed – Sir Stanley Matthews. The first professional ever to be knighted, the statistics of his career are awesome. Never sent off or booked, he played top class football for 31 years, retiring at 50, and last turned out for England aged 42. He was elected the first ever 'European Footballer of the Year', and twice was recipient of the English equivalent, the second time aged 48. More importantly, though, his skill levels were a wonder to behold – a genius, who filled stadia worldwide no matter what the weather; unique, his like will not be seen again.

50

Journey to the Big Apple

*F*OR the first time in our lives, Ann and I were destined to spend Christmas away from the shores of our 'sceptred' island; in fact, on another continent.

Matt and Avisa had invited us to share the festivities with them in New York – an act of great thought and generosity (though I was aware we would be required to help pacify some of the Yuletide exuberance of three vibrant, much loved grandchildren).

Now visiting family around our homeland poses few problems; Traversing the Atlantic, though, is a very different matter. Fortunately, I am married to a lady with great qualities in the fields of looking to the future and keeping calm. Thus was the planning and organising done by her – quietly and efficiency. I could not escape totally, as I needed to be involved in such matters as visas, travel insurance and the like. As to the first, the United States is possibly almost as difficult to get into as North Korea (though certainly easier to get out of). Fortuitously in this direction, we obtained the necessary documents back last spring when we visited them in the 'Big Apple', ones which still covered us for this trip. Travel insurance, though, poses problems; as we are both still under 80 and in tolerable health its acquisition is not too difficult (though, if an octogenarian, it would appear to be a minefield). No, the sting lies in the cost – one thinks of a seemingly fair price, then adds a nought. It had to be done though (after all, a visit to an American hospital to have a sticking plaster attached would possibly cost as much as a night in the Ritz).

Passports were the simplest of the requirements as ours were renewed just a couple of years ago – thus they will last us until probably our longest journey will be one to the supermarket (or a care home).

Currency, though – we would need that; thus a visit to my bank. A most pleasant lady was there to help; I explained my mission. 'Oh yes, we can order them for you,' said she. I was a touch taken aback – after all, I wasn't asking for the obscure such as Moldovan 'Leu' or Mongolian 'Tugrug'; one would have thought the 'almighty dollar' would have been available instantly in every branch in the country. I only wished for a minimal amount for the journey as Matthew, who can get a better exchange rate, would supply us with adequate funds when we arrived. 'I want just a few – but I do require them right away,' I pleaded. There was upon her face the expression of someone about to deliver grim tidings.

They did not come, for her colleague leant over, then whispered in her ear. Her face brightened; 'We do have dollars – sorry, I didn't realise.'

'Hallelujah! Well, all I need is 25.'

Her countenance again registered dismay; 'But they come in packets of 100,' she explained.

Presumably I wasn't myself that day.

Her tone suggested it would need a meeting of the Board of Directors at Head Office to give permission for this sealed carton to be broken. I thanked her, left the premises and headed for the Post Office. I knew the lady behind the counter and, seeing as they were busy, quickly got to the point. The request for a few dollars was made – and it was granted; I took out a wallet and extracted a credit card. From the good lady there came a glorious question, 'Do you have any identification, Ted?'

Bemused, I searched my pockets, but to no avail. Then I tried a debit card which, illogically, was instantly accepted. After well over an hour of hassle, I had managed to accrue enough 'bucks' to pay for a taxi, if needed, at JFK Airport.

Then there was the packing; Ann was very much in charge of this and did an awesome job. The clothes were no great problem – pack for warmth.

Presents, though – that was different. Ours is a largish family and seemingly all gave us gifts to take across the 'pond'. . . we needed a skip but Ann managed somehow to get them all in a case, albeit massive. Five days before the Yuletide, we set off. Good fortune was ours; there was no adverse weather, accidents, road works, heavy traffic on the motorways, no strikes, hold-ups or aircraft engine failure at Heathrow.

Thus, safely, we traversed the Atlantic; Christmas had begun.

51

Christmas in New York

*I*T is easy when living in these islands, members of a very independent, at times possibly introspective race, to feel there are customs and ways we pursue unique to ourselves.

Some are but probably fewer than we think.

Having said this, it's a fact that numerous relatively universal festivals, celebrations and events taking place world wide, vary enormously in detail, sometimes to an extent they bear little similarity.

In this direction, Christmas is well to the fore; across much of Europe habits and ways differ, while here in Britain we keep the event in our own long established fashion, one which mirrors, possibly, our heritage and foibles.

Recently we discovered, Ann and I, that the United States has its own approach to it all – effusive exuberance leading up to it, almost instant indifference once past. Indeed, it is easy to accept that which is often opined: Thanksgiving, to Americans, is more important, clearly more symbolic, than December 25th.

Still, I can report the revered, benevolent crimson-garbed gent who makes, an annual pilgrimage, is also to be found fit and well on the far side of the Atlantic, though there he is given a different name.

Usually we call him Father Christmas, but the Americans say 'Santa Claus'. Assuredly he was ubiquitous especially in the department stores; indeed he must have had a fleetness greater than Usain Bolt, so widespread were his appearances.

He certainly visited Matt and Avisa's home in New York where we were staying. On Christmas Day morning our grandchildren found stockings, almost the size of airport wind socks, bulging with an eclectic range of gifts.

Being true Brits, our son and daughter-in-law had a traditional Anglo-Saxon celebration – delicious fare devoured, carols played, along with games (from which, like illness, there is no escape), *A Christmas Carol* watched on television and Happy or Merry Christmas wished to one and all.

Peculiarly this is a term of goodwill rarely heard in many parts of the USA, especially New York.

Such is something of a conundrum. For here, predominantly, is a very Christian nation, yet it seems afraid to mention the name of the founder of the faith, the celebration of whose birth is the cause of the festivities. Inexplicably, they wish each other 'Happy Holiday', studiously avoiding the name of the Saviour.

Also, although according the Yuletide lavish attention and publicity, in effect, they recognise only the day itself. For while in our islands, the holiday period begins a week or so before Christmas and carries on beyond the New Year (some folk taking the entire period off), such does not happen stateside, where not even Boxing Day is a holiday.

A cynic might suggest that there the marking of this special time of year could be described as a triumph of brief sentimentality over true substance.

No such charge could be levelled at Matt and Avisa, however, for this annual festival was transformed by them into a magical one. Thoughtful quality gifts all round, abundant beverages for all tastes, warmth and goodwill to an extent that Ebenezer Scrooge would have been converted without the influence of the ghosts.

Ten days we were with them, boredom not an option; when not feasting or relaxing indoors, we were out and about in the Big Apple, walking, seeing shows, absorbing the ambience of a very different city and culture. Indeed, every time I visit the States, l am aware of the difference – despite historical ties – between the lands of John Bull and Uncle Sam.

The time sped by with a pace inevitable when life is being enjoyed; thus New Year's Eve saw us return to these rocky, historic shores. It had been a memorable sojourn for us both – one to treasure – with our family; ten days of comfort and relaxation spent with dear people who shrouded us in kindness, generosity, respect and love.

The highlights were abundant; there was a lowlight, however. From the basement of the house came a diabolical smell. A blocked drain? Worse – a gas leak?

The fire department were called; they were soon on the scene sirens wailing – four appliances.

Just as rapidly, the problem was solved; a dangerous hazard? No – an intruding skunk. It was removed. As for the weather? Well, we had a white Christmas – and the winds came from the Arctic.

52

Kids

'KIDS – what's the matter with all these kids today?' So goes a line in a popular song from a musical some years ago.

Another follows which enquires, 'Why can't they be like we were, perfect in every way?' Well, to be fair, I cannot claim total perfection as a lad. Truth be told, I was riven with faults, the majority of which have worsened with age.

However, I've managed to live without falling foul of the law – save for an occasion when my right foot was too eager caressing the accelerator pedal – have always secured regular employment (though with a number of bosses in a wide range of fields) and maintained, generally, a civilised relationship with my peers.

And the reason this flawed boy and youth grew up able to sustain civilised links with folk throughout a longish life? And has become a citizen with sufficient discipline to live within accepted standards?

Well it's nothing to do with personal attributes of any kind, but rather to my good fortune in having steadfast, loving, honourable parents. Simply, I was brought up to know right from wrong, to respect the views and entitlements of others and to attempt always to live by acceptable values.

Being raised by good people guarantees nothing, of course. Many of history's great villains had decent parentage yet the prospects of a girl or boy becoming a sound adult is vastly higher if they have the benefit of a mother or father (preferably both) who will prepare them for the rocky, hazardous nature of the path through life.

Personally I showed few qualities as a father – save I love my children (and now my grandchildren). Rather, to my shame, I was a delegator. I realised early in parenthood that I lacked both the consistency and resolute commitment to be a major success at it. So I left it to a lady who was, and remains, brilliant – my spouse, Ann.

That our four sons have grown up to be decent, honest, industrious men (also in the case of the three married ones, caring husbands and fathers) is down to her.

She was ever available to listen to problems, give sound guidance, instil ethics, rules of behaviour and, when they were young, she did not shy away from disciplining them if necessary. She was, and is, a role model when it comes to mastering the arduous art of raising a younger generation.

What relevance, you might justifiably ask, has all this regarding the question posed at the commencement of this ramble?

Well, it is a roundabout way of stating that, in my view, there is nothing wrong with kids today.

Probably there are no more children with delinquent tendencies in these times than there ever were. It could be argued, though, that often people find it harder to become adept at the arcane art of raising children nowadays.

To be fair, it is possibly more complicated for contemporary parents to guide their offspring towards fulfilling adulthood than it was for my generation. We live now in a more complex age where youngsters have access to, and are influenced by (at times, alarmingly so) computers, mobile phones, communication systems of almost chilling sophistication.

The wise counsel of many exemplary guardians is too often neutralised by the sedition which can be spewed forth via social media, a modern phenomenon which can be beneficial but which, also, can exert malign influence – bully, even terrorise.

The present day obsession with 'celebrity', where frequently fame and fortune comes the way of the outrageous rather than the talented and honourable, also sends confusing, mischievous messages to callow youth.

And the raising of children, difficult for two, is clearly even harder when, increasingly, it is performed by one – usually the mother. Granted there have always been break-ups of marriages and partnerships but the escalation of such has made life more fraught and insecure for children and the parent.

It could be, though, that in these times, there is a touch too much tolerance of indiscipline and bad behaviour. When a child disobeys a reasonable instruction, there can be no compromise, no negotiation.

Fairly, but firmly, they must be made to comply. A home with young children cannot be a democracy. Views, desires, even idiosyncrasies, of junior members should be listened to and respected, but the mother or father (hopefully both) must have the ultimate say; anything other is anarchy.

53

A Housing Shortage?

*I*T is said that in this country there is a major shortage of 'affordable housing' (a somewhat ambiguous term, one feels); in virtually all categories of dwelling for that matter, whether for sale or rental.

Prices being asked tend to be high, suggesting it is certainly a 'seller's market'. Yet, as an avid watcher of television crime and murder tales (also, being a touch gullible) I have come to the conclusion that there are areas in our land where there must be empty homes in abundance – many in seemingly most pleasant locations.

For example, Midsomer. Here is a leafy, attractive district (possibly in the Cotswolds), yet seeing as virtually every tale shows murder and carnage akin to trench warfare there must be a proliferation of domiciles of varying values in need of occupation.

It's not the only place either. How about Oxford? Not long ago we drove through the famous old university town and were surprised to find it so busy, for if the 'box' is to be believed the dreaming spires have watched over more than half a century of violent death and mayhem.

Back in the 1960s, Endeavour, as a young detective constable, attempted, with limited success, to stem the tide of violence. It was a crusade he carried on until the millennium after promotion to chief inspector – Morse. Throughout all this, while he was ever excellent at detecting the identity of the assassin, he seemed incapable of thwarting the cascade of slaying which engulfed the city.

Since his demise, law enforcement amongst the august colleges has been largely in the hands of Inspector Lewis, a genial geordie who, with his able assistant Sergeant Hathaway, has laboured to bring to justice the flock of murderers who throng the ancient streets.

This savage culling of the local citizenry must have led to many uninhabited homes – surely? Then there's Denton, where the irascible Inspector Frost attempts valiantly to dam the flow of corpses.

Unlike Oxford, the location of this town and Midsomer are not revealed, but wherever, the windows and filing cabinets of local estate agents inside these boroughs must be crammed with details of properties covering a range of prices.

There is, though, a crime series which, despite the community producing many assassins, would have seen few empty houses – there would, however, have been many blitzed ones. For in wartime Hastings – the setting for the splendid *Foyle's War* – the Luftwaffe managed successfully to eliminate abodes (innocent people, also, sadly) to such an extent accommodation of any kind would have been like gold dust. However, the cerebral chief superintendent Christopher Foyle – was still kept in constant action rounding up locally bred killers.

Back in the same era – also before in the 1930s and afterwards into the fifties, for that matter – that brilliant Belgian detective Hercule Poirot was exercising his 'little grey cells' to remarkable effect, almost always able to pinpoint the identities of the killers who decimated the populace; whilst during similar decades, the village of St Mary Mead appeared a lethal location in which to reside.

However, those responsible for such slaughter rarely got away with it thanks to the awesome sleuthing genius of an elderly local lady, Miss Jane Marple; like Poirot, her skills seemed vastly superior to those of the local constabulary.

Mind you, for many years Miss Marple's village (like Poirot's locality) must have had numerous empty properties so drastic was the culling, but since it all happened long ago the places probably have long since been repopulated.

This massive and long lasting (according to television) hurricane of massacre does have about it an aspect of democracy, for it is fairly spread amongst both genders, all incomes and throughout the country. North and south, detectives, professional and amateur alike (especially, these days, the former) are kept in full time employment.

Up in Yorkshire, there are that effective duo Dalziel and Pascoe, also Inspector Banks, whilst the redoubtable Hetty Wainthropp Investigates. In Northumberland, Inspector Vera Stanhope is a force to strike fear into the hearts of transgressors. Further north again in Scotland, the rather disagreeable Rebus ensnares the villains, having taken over from the more likeable Taggart, whilst here in the south west, Wycliffe has, until recently, caused many an assassin to be 'banged up'.

Still, whilst all these bastions of the law are, or were, an asset, it would surely be better for society if they were better at the prevention side of matters as opposed to the cure.

Mind you, it would not make for such enjoyable viewing, would it?

54

Memories of Youth

*H*AVING had a far longer past than I will a future, inevitably I reflect upon the, almost, eight decades I have lived on this earth, dwelling in this very special country of ours. Mind you, I do not view yesteryear through spectacles of a 'rose tinted' hue; ever imbued with a somewhat cynical, at times jaundiced view of this life, nostalgia is minimal, whilst that supreme mischief maker, sentimentality, is banned utterly.

Still, there is scope for distortion – majorly so – as memory, especially when one gets older, is amongst the most inexact of sciences. Born in the early part of the Second World War, my first recollections concern the end of it (or, at least, I think they do); for I feel reasonably confident that I can recall seeing the mighty bonfire that lit the sky above Bere Alston Recreation Field to celebrate VE night in May 1945, though to be fair, it may have been VJ night which took place some 3 months later. If my recall of those momentous celebrations is a touch fanciful, then my initial recollection – of which I am certain – would have been of the devastation of Plymouth.

It was just after the war; I was with my mother; we took the train from the Bere Peninsula (most journeys, north and south, were made in such fashion back then, the quality of rural rails being far superior to the highways), and arrived at Plymouth station. We walked up the hill to what is, now, a large roundabout with the centre of this great city, its shops, offices and streets spread out before us. Stood in that same spot, more than 70 years ago, though, mother and I were confronted with a vast largely open space; there was rubble, mind you, and in abundance, a small number of skeletal buildings, and a row of Nissen huts transformed into shops (truly the indomitable spirit of the British) – but the heart of the famous old port had been largely obliterated by the Luftwaffe.

One of those bombed buildings which still had some form was St. Andrew's Church. After its reduction to a shell, some citizen placed above the main door a rough hewn piece of wood upon which was carved one word, in Latin, 'Resurgam' – ('I shall rise again'); it did, along with the town around it. Indeed, despite being possibly (for its size) the most bombed city in Britain, most of its centre had been rebuilt before many like battered boroughs had even begun to reconstruct – a striking achievement.

The city was also the setting of an early calamity – well, it was to me. The Old Palace Theatre in Union Street was the location (a building still there, now looking rather sad). Most years my parents would take me to the annual pantomime which usually I enjoyed immensely. This one occasion, however, I did not. The show was well underway and, not unusual in pantos, performers came down from the stage and chased each other up and down

the aisles. They were about to pass where we were sitting
– but stopped, abruptly; my mother was sitting on the end
and upon her lap lay, just opened, a quarter pound box of
Cadbury's Milk Tray – in those austere times, a prize to be
coveted. The artistes grabbed the box, emptied the
contents into their mouths, returning it empty, then carried
on with their chase. The memory of this savage loss haunts
me to this day. That old music hall also looms largish in
another boyhood sorrow – though of less magnitude.

A fan of Laurel and Hardy films, my good Mum and
Dad took me to see this famous duo doing a live show; it
was not to be, as Oliver was taken ill that very same day
and was unable to appear; he was never to work again.

This all happened in the early 1950s, as did an event
burnt forever into memory; October 1952 saw my father
'imprison' me in Home Park for the first time; I've never
been able to escape since.

That same year saw the death of the much respected
King George VI – we were told of it at school. Then came
1953 – a truly significant annum; the Coronation of our
Queen, the conquering of Everest and, not least to me, that
glorious footballer, Sir Stanley Matthews, won his FA Cup
Medal.

These reminiscences of my childhood – the 40s and 50s
– are still vivid. Most of us can probably recollect with far
more accuracy that which happened in our early days than
the events of later times. Although much of the subsequent
60 years remain in my mind, clarity gets ever more
flawed, and a touch prone to illusion.

55

The Joy of Winter

*D*ESPITE being a man who could feel cold in a sauna, my favourite season of the year is, and always has been, winter.

Perhaps a touch like Dracula (though tea, coffee, wine and whisky are beverages I prefer to blood), I am something of a creature of the night; most certainly I hate garlic and, when looking in a mirror, witness a hideous visage.

Whatever, my spirits always rise on September 21 when the sun crosses the Equator moving south, and soar the last weekend of October when the clock goes back an hour heralding early dark evenings – which get ever earlier.

Why this is I know not – but then who can ascertain the reasons for personal foibles and idiosyncrasies? Even as a boy on the farm I was the same. Naturally I, along with my older brothers, was expected to help with the multiple tasks, year round, which dominate the daily round on a holding of 80 acres with a range of livestock and the growing of many crops, much of it of a horticultural nature. Winter, largely, was devoted to the care of animals, and I had no problem being out and about, even in stormy wet weather, or snow and frost, bringing in fodder for the stock, then feeding them (it's quite remarkable just how much a milking cow will eat and drink).

Summer was very different; the sun blazing down (well, at times, anyway), strawberries ripening rapidly thus requiring picking from the plants with some alacrity, to be punneted up and sent off from Bere Alston Railway Station to markets around the country.

The farm was alive with, largely, casual workers (mainly ladies) from the village, in peak season turning out in shifts; thus the working day lasted from six in the morning until late evening.

Even though I was not expected to put in long hours, being of a somewhat solitary and, in honesty, inactive nature, I disliked the often frenetic activity all around, the urgency of it all (though I still preferred farm life to school); my parents, however – my mother especially – derived much fulfilment from it, plus clearly it was a major part of their income.

Summer time, too, brought hay making. By its very nature, it could only take place in hot weather. A sweat laden, insect ridden business which never appealed – though I did enjoy regular visits to the large stone jar of 'Scrumpy' placed, traditionally, close to the growing hay rick (though the gents doing the work did not approve of a useless youngster like myself illicitly partaking of the potent brew). All of it, of course, was essential to the feeding of the animals during the winter months, but I didn't see it that way at the time. Indeed, I once said to my Father, trying to be clever, that I felt those who ate it should make it. He was unimpressed. Did my outlook and attitude improve with maturity? Assuredly not.

Going out with our family on a nippy winter's day could, to me, be pleasurable. Sitting on a local beach in summer, sandwiches laden with sand and flies, all tranquillity destroyed by multitudes stumbling around playing games, fetching ice creams, trying (usually unsuccessfully) to pacify hot, fractious children, is how I imagine purgatory. Summertime also puts you in danger (unless you really keep your wits about you) of having to suffer the tedious torture of that relatively modern monster – the barbecue. The allure of sitting on a hard, unsteady chair, rain threatening or bugs buzzing (possibly both), eating half cooked – or fully burnt – food, escapes me.

Even a visit to the dentist can be preferable – at least the chair will be soft.

The very long days do pass though – eventually. September arrives, the school holidays end, Westcountry towns and roads are returned to we locals – life becomes more serene and relaxing. Autumn is upon us – winter beckons. There are, though, mild traumas to be endured before it does; early October brings Tavistock Goose Fair; the end, that dire, largely American import, Hallowe'en. Granted November 5 sees another raucous do, but at least Guy Fawkes Night is totally home grown. After this – winter; cosy evenings, no gardening, less stress, fewer callers, darkness 'til past waking.

Mind you, there is, to be fair, one plus regarding the summer; no league football, thus no danger of suffering the 'slings and arrows' which hurtle one's way from Home Park.

Even a visit to the dentist can be preferable – at least the chair will be soft.

j

56

Phones & Social Media

MY parents having had the telephone installed when I was very young, I was brought up appreciating its value in terms of communication. So it was only natural Ann and I had one installed long ago when we moved into our first house together.

Now, those kind, resilient folk who valiantly read my meanderings are probably enquiring – so what? After all, the number of citizens in our great land who do not have landlines – and in these times, mobiles also – will be miniscule. The reason I state this is that, because of my terror of technology, craven approach to communication, ignorance of the Internet, my DNA of a dinosaur and, to an extent, passion for privacy, I have never moved beyond the basic invention of Alexander Graham Bell back in the nineteenth century.

Fortunately Ann has in that she possesses a cell phone – though she rarely uses it. Were it not for the fact the phone was part of my childhood, I would possibly be terrified of even that; my sole forward movement in the field of getting messages and such to fellow human beings would probably have been to upgrade my carrier pigeon – retiring an ageing one, replacing it with a younger, faster bird.

The folly of it all is that I am fully aware of my selfishness – the difficulties I cause others when they wish to have contact with me and, indeed, the unnecessary barriers I put in my own path when wishing to get hold of them. Not having a mobile, there is assuredly no texting to anyone either. To be honest, even if such advanced equipment came into my possession, I'd not have the slightest idea how to use it – and even less desire (plus, in truth, courage) to learn. Instead of employing my fingers on a key pad sending letters and words through the ether, I use them to operate the sophisticated gadget I carry in my coat pocket; 'Biro' is marked upon it and to deliver its output, I employ the excellent services of a longstanding organisation known as Royal Mail. Mind you, whilst I state all this in honesty, I am not unaware of the foolishness of such cowardice.

Also, I am mindful I am a hypocrite, for whilst with friends and benevolent colleagues I play the 'old dog, new tricks' card when it comes to cyber dread. I am rarely reticent when it comes to asking them to employ the Internet for personal matters – buying tickets, booking holidays, accessing data, obtaining facts via 'Google' and the like. Indeed, I rarely now risk a hernia by lifting down from shelves the mighty tomes of The Encyclopedia Britannica when requiring intelligence, thanks to the patient help of others getting data up on the screen; and if they did not, would I change my reactionary ways? No – it would be back to the weight-lifting and the, often, difficult scanning of fine printed yellowing lines.

Mind you, whilst I concede I cause myself and others problems due to my 'Luddite' ways, I take some comfort from the fact that I can never be tempted into the minefield (certainly potentially a terrifying one, it seems to me) which can be the territory known as 'social media'.

Facebook, Twitter, You-Tube, the wider Internet – all clearly play a huge, almost dominant part in modern dialogue and human inter-reaction; at their best their employment can bring so much benefit to the user – ease so much of the pressure of modern life. There is, though – as is so well known – very much another side, one pregnant with peril; a zone seemingly so often the terrain of the predator – those malevolent perverts, malcontents, deviants, degenerates and plain nasty whose aim in life, it would appear, is to cause pain, distress, misery, often real harm to others, frequently for the sole reason it brings to them malicious pleasure and twisted satisfaction. Such is made worse by the fact that these vile individuals pursue their merciless abuse under the shield of anonymity. Due to these cruel cowards, many lives are blighted – some ruined; indeed, there are those tragically driven to suicide. Mind you there are some who bring trouble to their own doors, men and women alike who put comments on social media – perhaps critical of others, or controversial in diverse directions – which can alienate colleagues, friends, even family; indeed, with politicians and celebrities, it can ruin careers.

Muddle headed die hard that I am, such a calamity will never come my way; nor will an annoying email; and I'll never have my rest disturbed by a mobile call or a text. Indeed, the more I think on it, this unsociable old moaner has not the slightest motive to change his medieval ways.

57

Planning My Funeral

*L*OOKING towards the future – an aspect of my rather chequered life and career that I have rarely been able to master – I have made a request to my wife Ann, and my family, which I do hope is not acted upon for many a long day; I have listed the hymns which I would like sung at my funeral.

Morbid? Yes, to some extent, yet it is probably helpful to them to know the music which will accompany me on my final journey on a trolley down the aisle. After all, a death triggers so many problems, issues, legal requirements, demands of those close to the deceased, it can only be of help to them to put in place a request as to the singing, perhaps readings and so on, which might be used at this, the deceased's final public appearance.

What people might say regarding the departed cannot, of course, be regulated or even influenced; nor should it be, though most folk exercise generosity of spirit (an immense amount in some instances) and speak kindly of some whose leaving of the world is not widely regretted.

Hymns though – that is another matter. Whether or not

the departed is now in another world gazing down (or up) on this one is, possibly, the greatest of unknowns, but if he or she is, it could be of some comfort that the service is punctuated by the singing of that which, in life, they would have appreciated most. For me, being a man of conservative, traditional tastes and habits, my desire is that the organ's rich tones envelop the congregation (entry being free, hopefully not too sparse), with the vibrant melody of time honoured hymns – and such are what they will be.

Not for me a final journey made to the likes of Elvis extolling the virtues of a *Jailhouse Rock* or even the sublime tones of the great Sinatra (although I would certainly have him with me on the Desert Island). To start with, there would be *Bread of Heaven* – a rousing anthem which during a rather dissolute youth, I would sing along with others, discordantly, in local hostelries late of a Saturday night when liquor was in and sense was out. This will be followed by *To Be A Pilgrim* – for two reasons; firstly, it is one I like, secondly it has strong connotations regarding my lifetime obsession with a football club based in Plymouth; indeed, one line gives prominence in powerful form to the character building aspect of following Argyle – '*He Who Would Valiant Be, Gainst All Disaster*'; there have been so many of those over the years though few, mercifully, at present.

Definitely included is the moving, mind concentrating hymn, essential to cup finals and funerals, *Abide With Me*. Written in the 19th century by the terminally ill Rector of Brixham, the Reverend Lyte, it is so very difficult to sing the words without moisture glazing the eyes.

Yet, essentially, it is an anthem of defiance, of positivity

– even of ultimate triumph, though this could only, possibly, be found in the next world. Such, at present, is my list to be played and sung at my demise; it could change a touch over a period of time – if time there be – but not radically. Possibly there would need to be one or two extras in reserve, to come off the 'subs' bench' if, say, the organist mislaid the music to any of the others. That evocative psalm *The Lord Is My Shepherd* would be a contender as would be that stirring hymn, *Onward Christian Soldiers*, the singing of which exercises the lungs and lifts the spirit; also, it was written, in the late 19th century, by a good Devon man, the highly accomplished Reverend Sabine Baring Gould, rector of Lewtrenchard – assuredly a 'man of many parts'.

A traditional funeral favourite is *The Day Thou Gavest Lord Has Ended* but it does not appeal to me; perhaps I prefer songs of praise to be a touch more spirited and powerful even though services for the deceased are times of sadness and mourning.

One that does appeal is *The Battle Hymn of the Republic* which contains lines which ever linger in the memory, none better than *'He is trampling out the vintage where the grapes of wrath are stored'*; certainly mind concentrating words – and it has a cracking tune. It will not be used though – it would not rest easy on the conscience of this patriotic Briton. The work of one American would be employed, however, the march *Semper Fidelis* written by John Philip Soma. Since time immemorial, Plymouth Argyle have taken to the pitch to this pulsating tune; with me, it would be played at the end of the funeral service – as I was leaving the field of play.

58

The But Syndrome

*I*T is only a three letter word; there can, however, be few
more mischievous – possibly even malevolent – and
surely it is hard to dredge up any which can better air
hypocrisy and prejudice; and the one syllable term? 'But'.

It proliferates and so often is used to mask meanness of
spirit – malice, vindictiveness even. To be fair, most of us
will use it at times and yet not be conscious of insincerity,
intolerance – possibly two-facedness. A while back, after
the membership of Muirfield Golf Club rejected the
proposal that ladies should be permitted to become
members, an opponent to female inclusion stated he
personally had no objection to women golfers, then
proceeded to mouth fatuous comments amongst which
was, 'But they take longer to complete rounds,' and so
forth. Subsequently, the vote was reversed, but probably
only because they were told that no major tournaments
would take place there as long as the ban continued, not,
one feels, due to a genuine change of heart.

A fellow I know – basically a pleasant, friendly gent –
voiced concern recently over the duo who had moved into

an adjoining house. 'I've nothing against gays,' he opined, 'but I don't want them living next to me.' Clearly he did have a problem with them, but had not the honesty to admit it.

A while back, a lady acquaintance – a charming person, ever kind and thoughtful, a devout, regular worshipper and helper at her local church – expressed views which, to me, exemplified the perversity of human nature. Discussing the unfairness and injustices of life, she expressed her disapproval of bias against any and all, with the words, 'We are all God's creatures,'; she ruined it, however, by the postscript, 'But I don't like gypsies.'

To be fair, I am guilty of such rather bigoted inconsistencies myself – and have been on numerous occasions. Recently a good friend voiced a view with which I had (and have) total sympathy; in the process he saved me from speaking likewise. As am I, he is a man well past retirement age but still working a goodly part of the week; similarly to myself, he enjoys it, stating, 'I'd hate not to work – I'd be bored and would miss the involvement.' He banished such positivity in an instant, however, with words bordering on anger – 'But then, having always worked in the private sector, I get little pension beyond the "Old Age"; if I didn't graft we would starve.' I nodded so vehemently in agreement, my head was little more than a blur. Thus an original statement of positivity had morphed rapidly into the voicing of a deep-rooted grievance, definitely a prime example of what could be termed the 'But Syndrome'.

The contrariness, prejudice and, often, selfishness of human beings ensures insincerity abounds; 'nimbyism' is fertile soil for this. 'I believe passionately in renewable energy but clearly the hills overlooking our home would be most unsuitable as a site for a wind farm,'; or 'more affordable housing must be built to enable young people to get onto the property ladder, but there is far more space the other side of town.'

On the world scale, it's sometimes opined that 'Action should be taken to destroy these wicked, murderous terrorists and the like – troops should be sent, but not ours; we've done enough already.' That's how it goes in so many fields of human activity. Often, though, such is followed by use of 'but' – the great disclaimer, the word which can absolve folk from actually having to pursue the basically sound, indeed honourable principles which they claim influence their lives.

Then there is what is probably the most regularly heard use of this three letter term – 'I'm not a racist, but. . .' This claim so often can be followed by assorted caveats which suggest that whilst the speaker may not be such in the worst sense of the word, they are prey to intolerance and bias.

Having said all this, I'm a hypocrite and sinner myself: I have respect for followers of all football clubs – but I have serious colour prejudice; I like only green shirts – but then only as long as they sport the Mayflower badge.

59

School

*I*T has long been an aspect of our family life which has bemused me, that our four sons, and their mother, my dear Ann, enjoyed going to school. Such a peculiar attitude would seem to have been passed on to the next generation; our grandchildren. And now, yet a further one, as our delightful great-granddaughter appears to love attending pre-school.

Mind you, looking back, my two elder brothers also had no horror of the daily incarceration in classrooms – and both, being intelligent, hard working lads, did well, nearly always, to use football parlance, up with the 'promotion pack' in the 'league table'. In fact, so accomplished were they, that Fred was the first person in the history of our family to go to university; subsequently he became a Geologist, ran a successful business and was highly regarded within his profession. Stan, coming from a farming family, wished always to follow this exacting way of life; he went to Agricultural College, then into practical work. He farms to this day.

Where, a long suffering reader might well ask, is this

preamble leading? Well, basically, to state that unlike the vast majority of my family, including my parents, I detested school – every minute, day, month of it. Not for me the smug adage, 'They're the happiest days of your life.' From the first moment of entering formal education, aged 5, until leaving it some eleven years later, I found it boring, oppressive, despotic; even, at times, intimidating.

Looking back, I've a feeling I was very much in a minority, as most of my school mates – boy and girl alike – appeared to gain fulfilment from those precious, character forming years of learning. Even the less keen generally lacked my self-destructive resentment at having to subject myself to this formal, at times rigid and strictly disciplined system (far more authoritarian than it is today).

In consequence – partly, at least – I did as badly as my brothers had done well. For whilst they had been high flyers, year in, year out, I was stuck in the 'relegation zone'.

I had been poor at primary school – a situation not helped, in my very early years (to my shame), by my all too often feigning of illness. For a while my dear, trusting mother believed me, but, due to my foolish habit of making a dramatic recovery just after it was too late to attend class, such soft hearted benevolence came to a halt – to my eternal benefit, of course, for it means I am able to read, write and have mastered basic numeracy.

Somehow I managed to pass the Eleven Plus exam (truly a mystery). Thus began five years and more of grievous underachievement at Tavistock Grammar. It's possibly a mystery my end of term reports were never forwarded to the Director of Public Prosecutions as they were dire to the point of being criminal, with often the most damning comments. In my defence, I'm not sure such remarks were always totally justified, but I would have to concede that my overall attainment during my scholastic career was lamentable.

There was one very happy day, though – the one on which I left this, to me, so restrictive life and entered the working world. It is now 60 years since that moment when I escaped what I saw as an educational penitentiary – albeit a civilised one; the greater part of a lifetime.

Now that I'm an old man, I find myself recalling this irrational antipathy towards school and assessing whether in this age I would approach my formal learning years in a more positive, open minded fashion. Sadly I've come to the conclusion I would feel exactly the same. Whenever I dropped my sons off at school, I did so with a sense of guilt, a belief that I was blighting their day. Plain daft, of course, but then my lifelong aversion to academia has been without logic.

For it is almost beyond understanding that whilst, in a long, highly varied, chequered working life, I've done jobs for which I've lacked all joy, I've never arisen from my bed prior to attending that place of labour with the foreboding which shrouded me, perpetually, when knowing I had to go to school. Do I regret this ludicrous lifelong phobia? Certainly. I spurned an excellent state funded education, which could have put me on the road to a satisfying, well paid career which would have made life more comfortable for my lovely wife and family.

If I could go back to my youth, would I be different? Sadly, most unlikely, as the dread remains – unabated.

60

A Mayoral Year

*B*ACK in the days of yore, when I had hair, my own teeth and did not require glasses, the Tavistock Town Council and thus in effect, the good people of the community, paid me a great compliment.

It was one which was assuredly not deserved – they voted for me, in May 1980, to be mayor of the old stannary town for the forthcoming year.

This article, I confess with a strong sense of guilt, is a reminisce – personal, parochial, perhaps even peripheral.

What has focused my meandering thoughts upon what, to me, were treasured days almost 40 years ago, is simply the fact that by a strange coincidence, I was asked by two different people recently, in the same week, a question which had never come my way before.

Clearly aware I'd spent very many years of personal inactivity and negativity as a member of the council, they enquired as to why I had never donned the chain of office which adorns the neck of the councillor who becomes mayor. The answer is, as stated; I was privileged to fulfil that role for 12 months, with the crucial and sublime support of my lovely Ann as mayoress.

That the two folk who made the inquiry did not know is understandable. One has lived in the area for under a quarter century, while the other would not have been born when the mayoral chair in the council chamber, almost large enough to seat King Kong, housed my more modestly sized posterior. The ceremonial robes are similarly vast, accommodating with ease even the largest mayor.

So almost 40 years back I was sworn in at the annual meeting of the council, while Ann was bedecked with the mayoress's ribbon and medallion.

Why I was so generously elevated to such a role I know not, but I will always feel grateful and honoured. Assuredly it was a year which, although half a lifetime back, will linger forever in the memory. Mind you, there is a vast amount to recall as there is no scope for boredom in this role – and no malingering.

From day one, life is dominated by civic, local and community events (plus, of course, we still had employment and heavy family commitments to attend to).

The summer months brought a manifold array of largely outdoor events to attend, in which active participation is often required. Fetes and fairs to open, a hectic though most enjoyable week involved in attending and judging events in the carnival; Races to start, art exhibitions to attend, folk and street dancing to set in motion and (purgatory for such an inept performer as myself) to take part in. Most terrifying of all, baby shows to judge (one mum ecstatic, the others outraged).

Then comes the autumn and winter seasons – civic dinners, local operatic and dramatic society performances, school prize givings, assorted concerts, twinning visits and the like – and Christmas. Carol services, shop window judging, nativity play enjoyment (heart warming – at times hilarious, even anarchic events are the latter).

Then, on Christmas morning, a customary visit to the local hospital – though I'm doubtful our call did much to aid their recovery. All year round, too, there would be the buying of draw tickets which occasionally produced a prize. There is a minus to the year, mind you – the proliferation of meetings. Being Mayor means you are automatically on all committees, and have to chair many (which means no skiving off half way through to watch *Midsomer Murders* or football on TV). Still, it is a relatively small price to pay for a sparkling, inspiring annum. For it is twelve months of deep, rich, rewarding involvement with the local community and an opportunity to meet folk of all backgrounds and ages who contribute so much and make this such a vibrant town and area.

Throughout there were moments and comments which still make me smile.

Among them was one which punctured any sense of self-importance, reminding me that whilst favoured by being permitted to wear the chain, I was but a servant of the people.

Having performed (at great length) a keenly anticipated draw at a pensioner's festive party, I was summoned to attend upon an elderly lady sitting at a nearby table. As I approached, she drew a pound note from her purse and thrust it into my hand: 'Nip down the street and get me some chips, Ted, will you?'

She was an elector – crucially, one living in my ward. Her wish was my command.

Of course, as an elector, her wish was my command –
puncturing any Mayoral sense of self-importance!